PRAISE FOR *THE HUNDRED STORY HOME*

"From the beginning of time, I believe it was ordained that Kathy would have a life-changing encounter with Denver Moore. He believed that as well. These unexpected encounters . . . thrill believers and encourage doubters to search. Prepare yourself to be thrilled or to begin searching for your Denver."

  —Ron Hall, bestselling coauthor, *Same Kind of Different*
   As Me (movie adaptation, October 2017)

"Compelling and convicting, *The Hundred Story Home* is a powerful testament to the way one person can affect transformation at the deepest levels. Kathy's beautiful storytelling propelled me outside of my comfort zones. . . . It's impossible to read *The Hundred Story Home* and walk away unchanged."

  —Courtney Westlake, author, *A Different Beautiful*

"Kathy has written one of the most inspirational books I've ever read. She weaves her incredible storytelling with authenticity and humility to the page unlike any oth—— K—th—— is ——— —f th——— ——— ———l— —h— ——— — need in their communities a—— —————— —— —————— ———— cause you to step out and d——— ——— —————— —————— —— he benefit of someone else."

  —Chad

"I LOVE *The Hundred Story Home*. Kathy Izard is a beautiful writer who has woven her personal life story into an account of her heroic effort to help the homeless. In her book of midlife discovery, she writes not only about creating a community for one hundred homeless adults but also inspires others to do so much more than what they ever thought possible."

  —Mary Dell Harrington, writer and cofounder, Grown & Flown

"This is a powerful story, skillfully told, and one that will hold you. As you read about a remarkable woman who gave up a promising career to do what for her was totally unexpected—to build a home for the homeless—you may find it is also a bridge to faith for you. As it has been for her."

  —Leighton Ford, president, Leighton Ford Ministries

"In *The Hundred Story Home*, Kathy Izard so beautifully and eloquently manages what we all wish we could—capturing her life story in a transparent and authentic way. Through the narrative of her life, we see Kathy's triumphs, struggles, and ultimate commitment to something bigger than herself: the call to help those less fortunate. Kathy is a storyteller, philanthropist, and courageous writer throughout these pages and in her life."

—Anne Neilson, artist and author, *Angels in Our Midst*
and *Strokes of Compassion*

"*The Hundred Story Home* is more than just a feel-good story of hope and purpose. It is an inspiring call to action, heralding the something-bigger-than-ourselves that resides within each of us. . . . It is this story and those like it that allow us to move beyond our perceived notions of the 'other' and embrace our abilities with humility, intention, and great purpose to solve the seemingly intractable issues we as human beings and as a culture say we care most about."

—Robin Emmons, CNN Hero and executive director, Sow Much Good

"*The Hundred Story Home* is a captivating, beautifully written account of one woman's search for purpose and how a combination of doubt, faith, and doing the right thing a thousand times over led to the building of something important and extraordinary."

—Mark Ethridge, author, *Grievances* and *Fallout*

"Compelling, inspiring, funny, and poignant. . . . This is a book about finding your purpose in a meaningful life; it's about faith and family and friendship. But mostly, it's a love story: a father's love, a mother's love, a daughter's love, and a beautiful, beautiful couple's love."

—Kristin Hills Bradberry, nonprofit adviser, Charlotte, North Carolina

"*The Hundred Story Home* is that book. The book that you can't mention off-hand and that you can't just hope someone reads. It's the book that deserves to be pressed into someone's hands with a promise to have tea and talk about it. *The Hundred Story Home* is the book that you'll be pressing into someone's hands because it presses into your heart."

—Rachel Estes, director of Missions and Outreach, Canterbury
United Methodist Church, Birmingham, Alabama

"Kathy Izard tells two compelling stories in one: about her journey toward fulfilling her life's purpose and about Charlotte's journey to finally treating its chronically homeless with compassion and dignity. Each has twists and turns, each has a happy ending, and Izard tells each with a style that will captivate readers far beyond her most natural audience."

—Taylor Batten, editorial page editor, *Charlotte Observer*

THE
HUNDRED
STORY
HOME

THE HUNDRED STORY HOME

a memoir of

finding faith in ourselves

and something bigger

KATHY IZARD

W Publishing Group

An Imprint of Thomas Nelson

Published in Nashville, Tennessee, by W Publishing Group, an imprint of Thomas Nelson.

Thomas Nelson titles may be purchased in bulk for educational, business, fund-raising, or sales promotional use. For information, please e-mail SpecialMarkets@ThomasNelson.com.

Scripture quotations are taken from the Holy Bible, New International Version˚, NIV˚. © 1973, 1978, 1984, 2011 by Biblica, Inc.˚ Used by permission of Zondervan. All rights reserved worldwide.

Poem stanzas from "The Journey" by David Whyte are printed with permission from Many Rivers Press, www.davidwhyte.com, © Many Rivers Press, Langley WA, USA.

Any Internet addresses, phone numbers, or company or product information printed in this book are offered as a resource and are not intended in any way to be or to imply an endorsement by Thomas Nelson, nor does Thomas Nelson vouch for the existence, content, or services of these sites, phone numbers, companies, or products beyond the life of this book.

ISBN 978-0-7852-2001-5 (eBook)

Library of Congress Cataloging-in-Publication Data

Names: Izard, Kathy, 1963- author.
Title: The hundred story home : a memoir of finding faith in ourselves and
    something bigger / Kathy Izard.
Description: Nashville : W Publishing Group, 2018.
Identifiers: LCCN 2017059535 | ISBN 9780785219880 (softcover)
Subjects: LCSH: Church work with the homeless—North Carolina—
    Charlotte. | Izard, Kathy, 1963– | Christian biography.
Classification: LCC n-us-nc | DDC 259.086/9420975676—dc23 LC record
    available at https://lccn.loc.gov/2017059535

Printed in the United States of America
18 19 20 21 22 23 LSC 6 5 4 3 2 1

To my Goose,
the First Believer

Sometimes everything
has to be
inscribed across
the heavens

so you can find
the one line
already written
inside you.

—David Whyte, "The Journey"

CONTENTS

CONTENTS

AUTHOR'S NOTE

The events in this book took place over the course of many years, the majority during 2007–12. I have reconstructed details to the best of my memory, using journals and e-mails. Some names have been changed to protect confidentiality. In several scenes the time element is compressed for the sake of narrative flow, but the stories told in these pages are true.

PROLOGUE

In 2007, a man I barely knew asked me a simple question that would change my life forever. The man was Denver Moore, coauthor of *Same Kind of Different As Me*, and he wanted to know:

Where are the beds?

For years after that encounter I would wrestle with why Denver had chosen to challenge me. At the time I was a wife, mother of four, graphic designer, and soup kitchen volunteer. How could I possibly do anything about Charlotte's homeless problem? Why would Denver imagine that I could?

But I finally realized the real question was, *Why had I listened?*

It has been said that the two greatest days in our lives are the day we are born and the day we understand why.

This book tells the story of my journey to why.

All those years ago I would not have argued with you if you said there was no God.

Today I would argue you are not listening.

one

SIX CANDLES, ONE WISH

We all must leave home to find the real and larger home.

—Richard Rohr[1]

It was the day I will always remember in the year I will always wish I could forget.

Standing on my toes and looking over the edge of her large green drafting table, I watched my mom carefully creating ten works of art. She was curled over in concentration so she could work closer to her pencil. We were in the spacious art studio added on to my parents' bedroom in our new split-level home. My family of five had just moved into this four-bedroom house on the last street of a new development on the west side of El Paso, Texas.

The art studio was a twenty-by-twenty-foot room with vaulted ceilings and natural light streaming in the windows. There were two kilns, easels, canvases, acrylic and oil paints, along with cabinets brimming with other supplies. A cassette player and boxes of classical music tapes filled the room with symphonies while we worked. My two sisters and I were probably the only three little girls encouraged to play Hallmark rather than house. For every relative's birthday, anniversary, or holiday, Mom got out the craft supplies and made us create custom cards. Glitter and glue weren't enough; we had to have a theme, an illustration, and a message, just like a real greeting card. I always thought of this space in our house as my father's love letter to my mom. This was the place where he wanted her to thrive even though she had been transplanted to desert soil.

El Paso was my father's hometown, and a decade earlier my mother had moved there from North Carolina out of pure love for him. All of the houses in our neighborhood were essentially ranch style with added western architectural elements: tile roof, adobe color palettes, and wooden beams protruding over arched windows. Kind of like the Fiesta accent package for Mr. Potato Head. Every front yard had a similar landscape of cactus and rocks—except ours. Mom had softened the rocks with the best of her home state, adding rose bushes and Bradford pear trees to our quarter-acre plot. I don't think the local nursery had ever heard of a Bradford pear tree when my mom insisted on special-ordering four.

As I watched her over her drafting table, Mom was deliberate in her work. Delicate fingers with rounded, clear-polished nails pressed firmly to steady the pencil as she meticulously sketched the wording on the outside of ten four-by-six-inch folded-over cards she had cut from white construction paper. This pencil outline was only a rough draft to ensure the letters were centered and evenly spaced.

Next, she took her deep black india-ink pen, slowly retracing the lines for the letters to emerge. As she finished one, she moved to the next until all ten cards proclaimed in perfect measured script:

You are cordially invited to celebrate the sixth birthday of
Katherine Grace Green

For weeks my mom had poured her substantial creative energies into devising a memorable day for me. Mom never remembered having even a store-bought birthday cake for her childhood birthdays, so she vowed that her girls would always know and remember their celebrations. She began by choosing a theme; everything my mother did had themes. The invitations, games, cake, and party favors all required matching motifs painstakingly penned, painted, and baked for the big day. Mom had decided this special celebration for my sixth year would have a cartoon theme. We had been saving sections of the comics for weeks, so Mom handed me the rounded craft safety scissors to cut out a six-inch-long section of the Goofy strip. I pasted it to the inside of a card and then added typed instructions that informed my best friend, Andrea, she was not only invited to my party but she must come dressed as this particular Disney character. Obviously, there would be prizes for best costume.

My mom had already let me pick my character. I chose Linus so I could carry a blue blanket and follow Snoopy (my friend Susie) around. My sister, Allyson, who was only a year and a half older than me, was obsessed with Disney princesses and wanted to be Cinderella so she could wear her blond hair in a bun and twirl throughout the party in a long blue gown.

My mom overruled this costume because Cinderella was not a comic strip, so Allyson unhappily dressed as Lucy from the Peanuts gang. My oldest sister, Louise, was twelve years old and already a lifetime away from wanting to come to her little sister's birthday party. Louise agreed to help babysit the partygoers but refused to be in costume, a huge disappointment to my mother, who loved to dress us in triplicate for church.

Finally the day arrived, and I could see from the kitchen window as my friends appeared at our front door. Andrea as Goofy, Nancy as Minnie Mouse, Beth as Beetle Bailey. Mothers and daughters filled our front porch, marveling over the creative costumes of the guests but, mostly, over the ingenuity of my mom.

"Lindsay, I swear, I don't know how you think of these parties!"

"I can't even draw a straight line much less do calligraphy!"

"I don't know how you have the time."

My mother deflected the compliments, gazing down, shyly touching strands of her chestnut-brown hair set firmly in place at the beauty shop with Aqua Net hairspray. Inside she was glowing with pride. Mom may not have been able to receive the compliments, but it was all true. She was an integral part of the PTA, officer in the Junior League, choir member and Sunday school teacher at First Presbyterian Church, wife and mother extraordinaire.

How did she do it all?

The party, as always, was flawless.

When it came time to blow out the candles, my friends pressed against each other to fit around our round kitchen table. The cake was another work of art baked by my mom. She lit the candles while my friends and sisters sang, "Hap-py birth-day, dear Ka-thy."

"Make a wish!" Mom said.

I hope I get an Easy-Bake oven.

Mom knew that's what I wanted. Tearing into my pile of presents, I spotted the rectangular box wrapped with pages of comic sections so even the gift would be dressed on theme. My own Easy-Bake oven.

This was the Best. Day. Ever.

As the last guest left, I could see the exhaustion in my mom's whole body, and I rushed to press my face against her legs, hugging her lower body as we stood in our front hall. The floor beneath us was a Lucite tile that looked like turquoise and celadon shells floating in a clear sea.

At that moment I truly believed my mother could walk on water.

She stroked the top of my wispy dirty-blond head, and when I looked up at her, she absently moved her fingers to straighten my bangs. Mom looked lost in other thoughts as her fingertips touched the fine hairs that didn't need fixing. Shifting her gaze from my hair to the six-foot countertop, Mom walked slowly away from me toward the kitchen to attend to some task I couldn't see. The counter held a green telephone the color of avocados, matching all the appliances in the kitchen, which were custom painted this exact shade of green. Beside our house phone was the week's mail piled next to her calendar, note cards, and Bible.

Mom held reverence for all three items—two of them to organize her short-term life and the other her long-term destiny.

She always tracked her duties on three-by-five ruled index cards, making careful notes with a four-color Bic pen, clicking the top to dispense the appropriate color. Mom picked up one of the white cards that ordered her busy world and studied the week's list:

Church—cotton balls Sunday School lesson
Jr League—committee coffee: bake seven-layer cookies
Ballet Carpool—Louise & Allyson
Thursday Kathy—party

Picking up her pen, she drew a line through the last item with only a hint of satisfaction.

"Well, that's done!" she said, trying to convince herself of the victory.

It was January 29, 1969.

Within six months my mother would be gone for the first time, and it would be sixteen years before all of her would return.

If I'd known, I would have saved my wish for something more magical than an Easy-Bake oven.

———

My dad never saw it coming. No one did.

My parents' old-fashioned love story began when they were college sweethearts and academic all-stars. My dad, John Leighton Green Jr., grew up in El Paso, where, in addition to being an all-state tennis player, he set a high school record for the highest GPA ever achieved. Dad did this while skipping two grades and finishing high school early at age sixteen. After graduation he traveled eight states away to attend Davidson College in North Carolina, where he eventually met my mom, who was attending Queens College thirty minutes away in Charlotte.

My mom, Lindsay Louise Marshall, went to high school in Winston Salem, North Carolina, and was equally gifted. Mom was top of her class, an all-state violinist, and a talented painter. She chose Queens because she was promised to her high school boyfriend, and he had been accepted to nearby Davidson. They agreed going to universities in proximity would keep their love alive until their inevitable marriage. My mom's parents disapproved of this boyfriend, so when the relationship ended her freshman year, Granddad said simply, "We've been praying for this for a long time."

She met my father during her sophomore year. Her friend arranged a blind date and they went to a movie in Charlotte. During this first date, my dad told her he was debating going into either the law or the ministry. My mom, who was rigidly religious and majoring in Christian education, told him flatly, "Anyone going into the law has no business being a minister."

Dad was not deterred by her opinion or by the fact that Mom seemed extremely uninterested in him. He arranged a second date and sent her a dozen red roses.

"Do you know why I sent you the roses?" my dad asked.

"Why?" my mom asked.

"Because I love you!"

"Well, I am not sure how I feel about you," she said, but Dad didn't give up.

Growing up, I used to be teased by my sisters about making "a Dad face" when I was really concentrating. A wrinkling of the brow, a narrowing of the eyes, and a clenching of the teeth. I can imagine my father making this face in his dorm room at Davidson, trying to decide how he would get this soft southern beauty to love him.

On Valentine's Day they went on a special date, and Dad was prepared. This time, he brought his Bible along and read aloud to her from 1 Corinthians 13: "And now these three remain: faith, hope and love. But the greatest of these is love."

She thought it was the most romantic thing anyone had ever done for her and that night told him, "I love you too."

They saw each other every weekend. One night, in a corner of the Davidson Kappa Sig house, Mom said, "You know I have no idea where El Paso is!"

"Why don't you marry me and then you won't have to wonder?" Dad replied.

That was how Mom found herself transferring to the University of Texas at El Paso in January of her junior year. My dad had graduated and was completing military service at Fort Bliss outside of El Paso. Mom would finish her degree in Texas and they would marry that summer. When they were packing her things in the dorm, Mom's English professor had chided my dad, "Don't you take her away from Queens until she graduates. She has one of the best minds I have ever seen."

Neither of them listened.

They married on June 9, 1956, the day after my father's birthday, because he said it was the best birthday present he could ever have. On their first anniversary and every anniversary and Valentine's Day after, Dad sent her another dozen red roses, and they would read 1 Corinthians aloud to each other.

Fully in love, Mom resolutely finished her studies at UTEP. During that drive to her new home 1,663 miles away from North Carolina, I am sure Mom thought hard about what she had done for love. The name El Paso refers to "The Pass in the Mountains," and the city itself wraps around the soaring but treeless Franklin Mountains. Cacti and tumbleweeds are commonplace, and there are more signs in Spanish than in English in this border town.

As foreign as El Paso looked to her, my mom never expressed regrets. My father was the answer to her prayers—the promise of a life filled with God, love, family, and service. She couldn't have foreseen the turns her life with my father would take. Dad switched from divinity school to law school and worked long hours toward his partner track. Mom appeared unstoppable in creativity, mother-hood, and civic responsibility. But that new home they had saved for years to buy would become the setting for a much different story.

That year of my perfect cartoon party, 1969, would be the year my mother's brilliant mind shattered for the first time—a blind-siding collision that left all of us with collateral damage.

two

DO GOOD. LOVE WELL.

Finding a sanctuary, a place apart from time,
is not so different from finding a faith.

—Pico Iyer[1]

Both my father and my mother would tell you it was faith that allowed us to survive the crash.

My parents were devoutly Christian, both from long lines of Presbyterian ministers and missionaries. My family went to church not just every Sunday but almost all day Sunday. There was Sunday school, then Big Church service, then afternoon youth group, and youth choir.

Every week in Big Church we sat in the same family pew in the First Presbyterian Church of El Paso. There was no plaque or official designation, but everyone reserved it for us anyway. We usually sat in the same order too. First, Poppa, a respected doctor in El Paso for over fifty years. He had delivered babies and then those babies'

babies, all while serving at the church and on the local school board. He was so passionate about public education that an elementary school eventually would be named after him, and every child in that school would carry a card to remind them of Poppa's famous motto:

You are as good as anyone; you are better than no one.

Nestled next to Poppa in the pew was Gigi, which stood for Grandmother Green. I adored her. She had enormous brown eyes set under a cloud of silver-blue hair. When she wrapped her arms around me, she would say my name with a playful twist: "Katarina, how are you?" And she truly wanted to know. Always. When she listened, she made me feel as though whatever I had to say was the most vital thought she had ever heard. In her presence, I always felt not merely loved but adored.

We all knew why. Although she was one of five children, Gigi was much younger than her four older brothers. By the time she was five, both of her parents had died, leaving her an orphan whom none of her brothers could care for. Gigi went to live with Grace Walker, from whom I received my middle name.

Grace lived on an estate where she worked as the caretaker of an unmarried heiress. While this was a luxurious setting to sleep in, Gigi grew up in this extravagant home where she was not quite family and not quite servant. She became part of a traveling entourage that moved every three months to catch the best climate in each of the heiress's four estates across the United States and Canada. Gigi was constantly uprooted from school. She grew up with few friends and no sense of family, describing herself a "poor little rich girl."

As a result, Gigi treasured the family she created: two sons, two daughters-in-law, and five granddaughters. My cousins lived in San

Antonio, so my sisters and I were the grandchildren Gigi spoiled weekly with sleepovers and long lunches. We would each get invited to her house for our own special dates, and Gigi would feed us her famous chocolate-mint sticks, a secret recipe she never shared, even when the Junior League wanted to put it in their cookbook.

I would curl up next to Gigi on her nubby pink couch and rub my fingers on the raised squares in the upholstery as I talked to her. Gigi patiently listened to all I had to say. She would hold my hand and look at me with those round chocolate eyes that gave her, even in her eighties, a perpetual look of childlike wonder. And she was always wondering. Wondering about me, my sisters, and, really, everyone she met. She truly wanted to know about a person—where you came from, what your story was—because she knew everyone had a story worth telling.

Next to Gigi and Poppa in the pew were my dad, mom, and us three Green Girls. Mom made me sit next to her so she could pinch my leg to keep me still if I started squirming. It was hard not to squirm in church.

Usually I kept my mind busy by staring up at the dark oak ceiling forty feet above my head and wondering how they changed the light bulbs. The timbers curved up in huge arcs on either side of a central beam, and it looked as if I were inside Noah's Ark, which had been flipped upside down. Light bulbs were not supposed to be what I was pondering. I was supposed to be listening to the word of God. But I never felt like he was talking to me.

I only behaved in Big Church because I knew the best part of the day, really the best part of my week, came after: lunch at Gigi's. My grandparents' home was tan brick on the outside with thick stucco walls and arched doorways on the inside. Stepping inside was like entering a sanctuary that smelled of roasted potatoes with browned butter. Gigi's weekly offering of lamb, mint jelly, potatoes, green beans with almonds, and angel-food cake with caramel sauce was a feast for my soul. It fed me more than any sermon.

Each Sunday we would gather for lunch at the dining room table while Poppa, who thought education was the most important thing a man or woman could have, always asked about our week, our lives, our future.

"Kathy, what's your favorite subject?"

"Allyson, tell me about your poetry."

"Louise, what colleges are you thinking about?"

Those Sunday lunches were not fast-food or drive-by affairs. We could easily be at the table for an hour and a half. And really, this was my Sunday school. Poppa discussing his work with the board of education, Gigi's commitment to the Junior League, Dad's service with the El Paso Cancer Treatment Center, and Mom's work with the Girls Club.

Mom used to take the three of us when she drove into south El Paso to do work with the Girls Club. To get there we had to drive along the interstate, I-10, which was bordered on one side by El Paso and on the other by Juarez, Mexico. The interstate ran alongside the Rio Grande River, the natural dividing line between the United States and Mexico. Translated from Spanish, Rio Grande means "big river," but the place where the river washes into El Paso is not grand at all. In most parts of the city, the river is a muddy twenty-five-yard trench—yet this river plays God.

Babies born on the northern side of the river go from hospitals to homes with electricity and indoor plumbing, luxuries unimaginable to babies born a mere fifty yards away on the other side of the river. Babies born on the southern side of the river live in shacks constructed of cardboard with dirt floors and lit by kerosene lanterns.

Mothers on the wrong side of the river risked crossing the border to work as housekeepers in middle-class El Paso homes, where they could earn ten times the available wages in Juarez. This meant leaving their families and going home to visit only every few months—if at all. Fathers in Mexico waded thigh-deep in water each day so they could work in construction or landscaping in El Paso and provide some semblance of a decent life for their families.

Growing up in El Paso, I experienced a sense of discomfort and even an inner shame because I lived on the "right" side of the river, born to the right parents and afforded the right opportunities. I also experienced a sense of helplessness about what happened on the "wrong" side of the river.

I suspect my father felt the same way. Maybe that's why my sisters and I weren't just raised to be good; we were raised to *do* good. In the early 1970s, when daughters in the American South were still being raised with the primary goal of becoming wives and mothers, my parents, especially Dad, expected more. He raised us to change the world. His refrain to me was, "You can do anything, Kathy, really anything."

I cannot recall a single conversation with my father about marrying or having a family. We talked about college, career, and the ultimate goal—leaving the world a better place. Dad wholeheartedly believed each of us would do just that.

It didn't seem to matter to him that we were being raised a little off the grid in West Texas. Dad just accepted on faith that we would all leave El Paso someday to make an indelible mark on the world.

While I may not have learned much in Big Church, I did take lessons from my childhood Sundays. I believed in two commandments. One from Dad: Do Good. The other from Gigi: Love Well.

three

NO CASSEROLES FOR CRAZY

Here is the world. Beautiful and terrible
things will happen. Don't be afraid.

—Frederick Buechner[1]

That El Paso landscape so startlingly close to Mexico imprinted on me not just an unease of privilege, but also an unease of the desert.

When there is no wind, deserts appear ancient, solid, immovable. But deserts are also deceiving. Unpredictable, remarkable natural phenomena occur there: mirages, flash floods, sandstorms—wicked sandstorms.

Once, while I was in the first grade, my elementary school closed due to a particularly vicious sandstorm. Our mothers had been called to pick us up early, so we each waited in our classrooms several hundred yards from the parking lot. Our teachers formed a human chain to safety, bending in the violent winds while stretching long ropes in their hands. As our names were called, we left the comfort of our classrooms to clutch the one-inch-thick lines leading to the waiting cars. Along the way, we stopped to wipe our eyes, stung by the swirling sand.

The morning had been clear with no warning that this drama would unfold. As I look back, what happened in my own home felt remarkably similar to this sudden, unanticipated storm.

In the spring of 1969, three months after my perfect birthday, the first signs of trouble began to brew inside of my mother's mind. She must have felt the winds stirring, and she tried to keep her world in order. Her first line of defense was the ever-present three-by-five notecards and four-color pen. As careful as a meteorologist tracking the currents, she would organize her thoughts into a logical order with perfect penmanship:

Groceries
    Orange Juice
    Pepperidge Farm Bread
    Jolly Green Giant Green Beans with Almonds
    Chicken
Carpool
    Tuesday—Jazz and Ballet, Louise, Allyson
    Wednesday—Piano, Allyson
    Thursday—Ballet, Kathy
Cards
    Anniversary (Johnson)
    Birthday (Karen, Anne)

Clear. Careful. She would make no mistakes. Her home, her daughters, her friends all needed tending. Dinner to be made. Carpools to track. Cards to send. There were always the cards. No matter how she was feeling, my mother was anchored in her

Hallmark habit. Buying and sending greeting cards was a staple of her domesticity and a grounding force in her days. We girls had to make cards in the art studio, but my mother purchased all of hers from Hallmark. Each week she would faithfully mail greeting cards to mark birthdays, anniversaries, and major holidays for countless friends and relatives.

My middle sister and I were in-house buddies and best friends. Allyson's imagination was limitless, and we would be fairy princesses or magic pixies in kingdoms and faraway places.

We kept our treasured collection of doll-sized evening gowns, daywear, swimsuits, and accessories in a small suitcase. We spent hours stretching the sparkling fabric over the impossibly perfect plastic figures, losing time in the magical land where our orange shag carpet in the downstairs den became a beach on faraway islands. One afternoon the sun we created from the den lamp burned a hole in Barbie's skull because we left her basking against the bulb all day.

Louise rarely played with us anymore, and on this day she was upstairs with her two best friends whispering secrets we couldn't fathom. Louise was the exotic animal who lived in the bedroom next to mine but never spoke to me. She sprayed herself with Jungle Gardenia perfume and went on dates with handsome cowboys, and I desperately wanted to be exactly like her. Or at least have her notice me.

Looking up from the wonder of Barbieland, I could see my mom outside in the backyard garden. The upside-down nest of her beauty-shopped hair was just visible in the rosebushes as she moved intently through the leaves, oblivious to the thorns. Mom held clippers, but she seemed to have no clear purpose among the bushes. I could see her lips moving as she walked through the garden, so I stood up to see if she was discussing something with the neighbor.

There was no one there.

Allyson and I cracked the back door to listen to what my mother was saying. She moved earnestly from bloom to bloom, speaking only to her beloved roses.

As we watched her, Mom at times appeared to see our faces, visible between the den curtains. But she looked through us with no apparent recognition.

"We need to get Louise," Allyson said.

As we rushed up the den stairs toward the kitchen, we were confronted with other signs of disarray—an open can of frozen orange juice concentrate melting on the kitchen counter and dripping to the floor, old hatboxes taken down from the bedroom closet and left opened and abandoned. Mom was always meticulous in her housekeeping, but now the house was a tornado of confusion.

We pounded on Louise's door until she finally opened it a crack to peer at us with disdain.

"What?!"

"It's Mom! Something's not right," Allyson cried. As she spoke she began to sob, and I stood behind clutching her arm, nodding.

Louise rolled her eyes.

"Really, Louise, you have to see!"

Louise followed us down the hall, stomping heavily, but when she saw the floor of my parents' bedroom strewn with orphaned hatboxes, Louise froze.

"There's more," Allyson assured her.

We hurried down the front stairs, pausing to observe the orange juice pooling on the linoleum.

Perhaps the most obvious sign of Mom's distress was the state of her desk, which took up part of the kitchen counter. The perfect script of her index cards was illegible and unintelligible:

Store
Lyrics songs
Silver-bife
Lucille Snoopy

"Where's Mom?" Louise asked urgently.

"With her roses!" Allyson cried.

We hurried down the short flight of split-level stairs into the den. Mom was still visible outside, moving in small circles through the rose bushes and speaking rapidly to her planted children.

We watched together, the Green Girls, trying to understand. How could this be our mom? My mom noticed when a hair in my bangs was out of place, but this woman didn't even see me, didn't recognize her own daughters. I looked pleadingly at my big sisters for answers. Mom's behavior had no context. She seemed to have come untethered from us.

Louise ran across the den and took the small flight of steps in two desperate leaps. Ally and I held hands, racing behind her. Louise grabbed the kitchen phone, pushing the buttons from memory.

"Gigi, this is Louise. It's Mom. I don't know what's wrong, but you need to come—now!"

We huddled together waiting for Gigi and watching Mom, who was oblivious to the chaos she'd unleashed.

Gigi arrived and convinced Mom to come inside. Dad rushed home from the office. Shaken with sorrow and confusion, he helplessly held Mom's hands, speaking words of love to a stranger who did not appear to hear him. Poppa met them all at the hospital with his thirty-year-old cracked black leather medical bag, but there was nothing inside that could heal my mother.

Mom spent that night at the hospital, the first of many she would endure on a psychiatric ward that in the late sixties and early seventies offered little respite and certainly no remedies.

I retreated that night to my secret hiding place at the top of my closet. The space was just wide and tall enough for a six-year-old to sit and dangle her feet over the edge. It was my indoor tree house where only my stuffed animals were allowed. I curled up on the shelf and hugged Snoopy, wondering if Mom would ever come home.

The suddenness of her affliction shattered us.

When Mom came home after several weeks, she was deflated and lifeless. She slept, it seemed, for almost as many days as she had been gone. My sisters went to camp that summer, and I went to stay with my aunt and uncle in San Antonio. At the time, I thought it was a vacation with my cousins, but I came to understand later it was because my mom still couldn't care for us.

That hospital stay was the first of many. Sometimes I wouldn't see her for weeks. Gigi, Poppa, and Dad would whisper in the kitchen.

"Exhaustion."

"Fragile constitution."

"Lindsay always tries to do too much."

With each episode the worry deepened. Poppa, a general practitioner, consulted psychiatrists and psychologists. In the early 1970s, these doctors had trouble naming my mother's condition.

Nervous breakdown. Schizophrenic form psychosis.

It would require the right doctor, the right medicine, and the right diagnosis—bipolar disorder—to truly bring my mom home to us. It would also take sixteen years.

During that agonizing period, each time as inexplicably as Mom went away, she would return. With each recurrence, however, a little more of her had blown away.

And each time a little more resentment built inside of me. Why did she sleep so much? Why didn't she just wake up?

When Mom unraveled, so did our family. She was the thread

that pulled us tight, and each time she left for a new treatment or hospital stay, we frayed a little more.

A housekeeper, Maria, came from Juarez to live with us, crossing the river illegally and staying for weeks at a time before risking the perilous journey back to visit her own two children. Maria had been trained as a secretary in Mexico, but she made more money in the United States cleaning homes. She was diligent at keeping our house, folding our laundry, and making our beds so it always looked as if everything was in order. But Maria couldn't care for us. She spoke no English, so we could only pantomime our needs to her. I had begun learning Spanish that year in first grade, but I never found a good translation for, "I want my mom back."

Gigi's house became my safe haven. Between the chocolate-mint sticks and the pink nubby couch, I found the place of comfort that would wrap me in reassurance. Our house, that perfect split-level ranch my parents had saved for to hold our dream family, became only a container that held our sadness. When Mom was depressed, the symphonies that had soared from her classical cassettes were silenced. The art studio was shuttered and dust collected on her paintbrushes as she slept, trying to outlast the darkness that settled over her for months at a time.

Throughout elementary school, I tried not to be needy. Dad was overwhelmed with his law practice and negotiating this new world of caring for my mother. I packed my lunch, walked to school, made all As, and walked myself home. My parents' bedroom door became a sign I monitored closely. It was the first thing I checked when I came in from school. If the door was open when I got home, I knew I would find Mom painting in the studio or tending to her roses. If it was closed, I would know to get my own snack, and she would wake up in time to make dinner. Mom always made dinner. It was the one task she never gave over to Maria—the one that still meant she was the mother in this home.

But the sight of her bedroom door closed when I came home became a wound that would not heal. I wanted her to want to wake up and ask me about my day. About the boy who had teased me on the walk home. About the play I was going to be in. I wanted desperately for her to be the superhero mom she used to be, but with each break that ended in a hospital stay our old life felt more like a TV show we used to watch. Someone had switched the channel in our lives from *The Brady Bunch* to *The Twilight Zone*, and we couldn't find the remote control to change it back.

Even when we had a name for this thing that had stolen our promise, manic depression, we still did not name it. We did not talk about it all. My dad. My sisters. My grandparents. We didn't comfort each other, cry about our devastating loss, or curse the diagnosis. We simply carried on. Dad went to the office every morning and still expected the three of us to do very well at school. I kept collecting As and added to my résumé student council representative, National Honor Society, and yearbook editor, but I never talked to my teachers about my home. I never said I had done my homework after visiting my mom on a psychiatric ward. I never admitted to my friends that the reason I never invited them over to my house was because I was afraid they might see my mother asleep in the middle of the day or, more unexplainable, manic.

I, like my family, simply became numb. I could no longer cry when my mom went to the hospital. She just did. I could not get excited when she came home. She would go back. The only cure for this pain was simply not to feel, not to hope.

By high school, I needed small escapes from this dysfunction and I found it by secretly rebelling at night. Andrea, a.k.a. Goofy, was still my best friend. Some weekend nights we would drive

22

over the border to Juarez to party in clubs that asked only for our American dollars and not our IDs. I was escaping the crazy in my home and she was escaping the cancer in hers.

Andrea's father had been battling cancer, and her mother was trying to keep the family business going while radiation burned new holes in their lives. It was striking to see how her family was supported as her father suffered. Their family was inundated with help, especially from their small Lutheran community church. Friends swarmed the tragedy with cards, meals, offers of compassionate support. I often went to Andrea's church on Sundays. The pastor called her father by name in the prayers and asked for his healing.

Unlike Andrea's family, mine was not showered with care. Throughout those sixteen years of our searching for a cure for my mother's mind, our fellow Presbyterians didn't bake and didn't write. It wasn't that they didn't care; it was because they didn't know.

We never told them. Whether Mom was sick or well, the Green family still went to church every Sunday, smiling at the friends around First Presbyterian Church, saying hello but not speaking our truth.

Mental illness doesn't work like cancer.

There is no Hallmark card for, "I'm sorry your loved one is bipolar."

There are no casseroles for crazy.

Over the years I watched Poppa, Gigi, Dad, and Mom all bow their heads in church, and I could make less and less sense of it. When I sat quietly in the pew beside them, I wasn't drawing on my program or gazing at the ceiling anymore. I was studying the profiles of my parents and grandparents as they prayed.

What exactly were they praying for?

I had no idea. But from where I was sitting, God had not answered any of their prayers, nor was he delivering us from this evil.

four

HEADED FOR HOME

Don't forget—no one else sees the world the way you do,
so no one else can tell the stories that you have to tell.

—Charles de Lint[1]

It was almost my last year of high school before any doctor could begin to explain what had happened to my mother's brain and the two keys to living well with a bipolar disorder. One, Mom would always need daily medications to balance her brain chemistry, and two, she would need to fight daily for her sanity.

He explained it like this: "When the mania begins, it is as if there are three TV stations and two radio stations all broadcasting her thoughts in her head at the same time. She has to constantly try to turn them down and figure out what she is really hearing. You are lucky your mom is so smart and can determine what is real. Most people can't—or they give up trying."

By my college years Mom had almost fully returned to us, as

had her early promise of a life of service, church involvement, and even classes to obtain a master's degree in art. Battling for sanity had swallowed almost two decades of her life—time she calls her Lost Years. Even after she was stable we held our collective breath, hoping not to tip the fragile balance that kept her with us.

I was not fully ready to appreciate her struggle. Although my mom was back, I didn't really welcome her into my heart. At twenty-one I could still revert to my six-year-old self, hurt that she had virtually disappeared after my perfect cartoon birthday and effectively left us wandering in the desert.

The self-reliance learned during elementary school was now almost pathological. I didn't want to depend on anyone for anything. If I craved that perfect home and family, I was going to have to build them on my own. And I was not going to look for a future in El Paso or even the state of Texas.

I worked every summer taking extra classes along with a part-time job at a design firm so I could graduate early from the University of Texas at Austin. At twenty-one, I was eager for adventure and desperate to leave the state I had always lived in. In 1985, I did. Watching it recede in my rearview mirror, I was not even a little bit sad.

Thirty years after my mother's odyssey from North Carolina to El Paso, I made the exact trip in reverse: Texas, Louisiana, Mississippi, Alabama, Georgia, North Carolina. The states fell behind me as I headed from the Texas desert to the green of Charlotte for my first job out of college as an art director with an ad agency. I was hoping it was the promised land.

In moving to Charlotte I wasn't trying to trace my parents' college path; a job offer in the same city where my parents had met was coincidental. It was also unplanned that I had ended up with a BS in advertising from UT Austin. I had started out at my dad's alma mater intent on going to his same law school, but my sophomore year, I took an Introduction to Advertising class just because it would be an easy A. As it turned out, watching my mom develop themes for parties and designing my own Hallmark-style cards had resulted in the skills I needed for mastering copywriting and graphic design. Advertising was apparently in my DNA.

UT's advertising program was run by Dr. Leonard Ruben, an original *mad man*.

"Concept, people, concept!" Ruben would yell at us. "What is your big idea? Why should I care about your product?"

Ruben didn't care what our mock ads looked like. He said it didn't matter how much you polished something; it could look good, feel good, but every ad concept had to have that intangible thing that separated it from everything else. The big idea.

Each week Ruben would bark out orders to us, demanding perfectly rendered two-page magazine layouts for a real product. This was twenty years before Apple computers and Adobe software would revolutionize our industry, so we typically had three days laboring with markers and layout paper to dazzle him. By the time I had been in the program a year, I forgot all about my law degree and my dad's approval.

I wanted Dr. Ruben's approval.

On the mornings that assignments were due, we would file into the classroom and pin our layouts to the wall with silver thumb-tacks, then wait for the Ad God to arrive. Gruff, bearded, and chain-smoking, Dr. Ruben would study our layouts one by one, slowly drawing in smoke and exhaling an impossibly long time later. For projects that were simply bad, he would slowly shake his head and rip a page from the wall. But for those layouts that completely lacked the crucial big idea, he carefully touched his cigarette to the edge of the paper and watched with satisfaction as the assignment disappeared into ash.

In the early days of the program it happened to me over and over. "Where's the concept, Green?" he would bellow.

Slowly I got it. We all did. And job offers waited at the end of this pilgrimage—mine in Charlotte.

In those days this southern city had a Mayberry feel—it seemed everyone knew each other and said *Hey!* In the beginning when strangers were friendly, I assumed they knew my parents. Then I realized it was just what people in the South did. *Warm* didn't just describe the weather; it characterized the way of life. People genuinely cared about talking to each other.

In 1985, a little more than three hundred thousand people lived within the Charlotte city limits, but it was already becoming a financial center that would grow to 2.5 million people in the metro region a decade into the twenty-first century. The same reasons I was attracted to Charlotte were drawing thousands of others: jobs, low cost of living, good quality of life. Unlike my advertising-school friends who shared cramped walk-up apartments in New York City, I could rent a brand-new one-bedroom apartment in a complex with a swimming pool. A ten-minute commute along tree-lined streets brought me into a laid-back downtown that consisted of a few dozen towers.

Starting my job, I was in heaven. It was everything Dr. Ruben's stories had promised—photo shoots, filming with TV crews, deadlines, and brainstorming. I felt glamorous at twenty-one with my own client roster and the responsibility to create regional and national campaigns.

Three months into my new career, I had barely looked up from my layouts. I knew only a few people in Charlotte, and my one friend was the boss's daughter, who worked in the marketing department. She invited me to a party but I declined, citing a client deadline. It was ten o'clock on a Thursday night, and I was still hunched over my drafting table when it hit me: I really needed to have a little fun.

By the time I arrived at the backyard party, my resolve to play a little was slipping. As I approached a small white house, the beach music blared, and a mob of friends danced the dance of a happy keg crowd. The yard was filled with strangers who all seemed to be friends from Chapel Hill or Duke. I was a transplanted Texan with no real connection to any of them.

Searching for the keg to drown my fear, I saw him: one tall figure, three inches above the rest of the crowd, facing sideways—a profile to my stare. Beer in his hand, he seemed part of the crowd but still somehow separate. He turned and caught me staring. I didn't look away. I wanted him to see me. When he did, I somehow felt as though I recognized him. Like we had always known each other.

"Beer?"

As he filled a clear plastic cup for me, I discreetly sized him up.

He handed me my drink and his lips moved, asking a question. But he was six three to my five three, and I had to stand on my toes to hear him. Somehow, with him leaning over and me stretching up, we talked for two hours, oblivious to the crowd that moved around us.

It was way past midnight before I remembered the unfinished layout on my drafting table and reluctantly drove home to my apartment, thinking about him all the way.

I knew little about him except that I wanted to know everything about him. A thought as crazy as the impulse that had sent me to that party would not stop whispering, *That's the guy I am going to marry.*

We had made no plans to see each other, but he mentioned in our awkward shouting conversation that he exercised after work every day at the YMCA.

The next day after work, I joined the Y.

Two weeks and fourteen aerobics classes later, I finally saw him again. He crossed in front of my car in the Y parking lot as I was leaving, holding his suit in one hand and his briefcase in the other.

I slowed down as he moved toward my open window.

He bent down to look in. "Oh, hey." A little confusion and then a flicker of recognition. "It's you!"

I tried to act casual and aloof. "Yeah! We met at the party, didn't we?"

"Yes!" Obvious relief appeared on his face now that he could finally place mine.

A prolonged, awkward moment passed.

Finally, he spoke. "You wouldn't want to have a beer with me, would you?"

We had a beer, then dinner, then another dinner, and then dinner every night for six weeks straight.

As crazy as it seemed, after only forty-two days of knowing him, I said yes to Charlie Izard's proposal, blurted out with no ring over a late-night bottle of wine. We were married within the year. Although I was happier than I had ever been, I also clearly remember a moment of panic at our rehearsal dinner, looking at his friends and family and realizing that they all knew Charlie better than I did.

five

A HEART WITH A HOLE

Making the decision to have a child—it is
momentous. It is to decide forever to have your
heart go walking outside your body.

—Elizabeth Stone[1]

I didn't just love Charlie from first sight; I loved his whole family too. It seemed by moving to North Carolina I had accidently stumbled into the life I was looking for. Charlie came from the type of big, boisterous family I had always envied. He was the middle of five children his mother had delivered in six years. Boy, girl, boy, girl, boy. His parents had been next-door neighbors in Asheville, North Carolina, but because they were eight years apart they didn't really know one another growing up. They rediscovered each other years later, and their five children eventually became part of a large family on both sides. There were so many cousins, uncles, and aunts that

Charlie had to draw a family diagram for me when over fifty of them arrived in El Paso for our wedding.

When Charlie was six years old, his parents settled into a picturesque gray clapboard on two acres of gorgeous gardens in Rye, New York. The first time I visited this childhood home I felt like I had entered the pages of a magazine ad for family nirvana. While I sat in their cozy kitchen, his mom cooked a lavish sit-down dinner from family recipes, his father breezed in and out depositing fresh-picked vegetables, and a golden retriever and two dachshunds wagged for attention at my feet. On the wall next to the dinner table was a framed illustration drawn by a friend depicting Charlie's family. In it, children played silly games in the driveway, animals ran pleasantly amuck, and his parents were hilariously and lovingly orchestrating the chaos.

Studying that drawing filled me with a kind of longing I couldn't quite name. Looking at all that carefree love and laughter spilling out of the characters, I could see the enormity of what my family had lost. The normalcy of Charlie's home brought me a sense of peace and safety that felt luxurious. It seemed in finding Charlie, I had also found an entire family. Although it was a place I had never been, it felt like I had come home.

I wanted to study it. Bottle it. Whatever had made that house a home, I was determined Charlie and I would recreate it for our family-to-be.

Three years after our wedding and three days before my twenty-sixth birthday, our first daughter, Lauren Lindsay, was born, followed seventeen months later by her sister Kailey. We decided one more child would create the perfect family of five, but I had trouble getting pregnant this time, so my ob-gyn ordered an ultrasound to check for a cyst.

"Yep, there's two," said the ultrasound tech, who was not supposed to say anything to patients.

"Two cysts?" I asked.

"Two babies!" he said as if I was an idiot.

"Two babies? I'm not pregnant."

"Oh, yes, you are," he said, "with twins!"

Fraternal girls, Maddie and Emma, completed our family of six. With the twins born, Lauren and Kailey never needed to play with dolls again. They had live ones. With one sister for each of the older girls, there were endless games and possibilities. Maddie and Emma grew up being dressed up in outlandish costumes, carried precariously on piggyback, and offered potions of twigs, leaves, and mud concocted in the backyard by their older sisters. They were a growing, laughing pack with seemingly one body, eight legs and four hearts. One call—"Laurenkaileyemmamaddie!"—could bring them thundering down the stairs to dinner, a twin dangling from each older sister's arms.

Looking at the four of them sometimes caught me off guard. I couldn't believe they were ours. That we had created this blond bundle of beautiful girls.

Their antics and giggles began to create in our own home an image like the one on Charlie's family's kitchen wall. Now we lived in a picturesque home ourselves, around the corner from Queens College (now Queens University), where my mom had first gone to school and met my dad.

Charlie and I settled into a rhythm of the daily basics needed to care for a family of six by dividing and conquering the duties. Although I chose to stay home, I didn't want to give up on a career, so I started a graphic-design business out of our house, designing logos and brochures during naptime or after the girls went to bed. We used plenty of babysitters, but I wanted to be the one they came home to after school. I wanted to be there to ask them about their day. I promised myself our house would never break. It would be like the "before" in my childhood home. I would keep my girls safe, and we would be whole always.

I remembered how Gigi had so easily curled up with me on the couch to hear my problems. It was the most natural thing in the world for her to listen and love me and my sisters. But I realized it was very hard for me to do the same. I just wanted to fix things for my girls so they never had to cry or feel sad. Watching one of my daughters feel pain was agonizing to me. I had no idea that being a mother would be so heart-wrenching.

Maddie and Emma had been born six weeks prematurely, with Emma coming in a little over six pounds and Maddie barely registering five pounds. While Emma was a chubby little baby, Maddie remained much skinnier and smaller than her sister. At first, we weren't concerned because Maddie was achieving every developmental milestone before Emma—smiling, standing, crawling. She was a tiny bundle of energy who never sat still and hated to nap. When she finally fell asleep at night, hers was a pass-out slumber like someone had pulled her power cord. But at their nine-month checkup, Maddie weighed only fourteen pounds and the pediatrician was alarmed.

"She is meeting the criteria for failure-to-thrive syndrome," he told me after consulting her chart.

We'd been watching Maddie carefully ever since her doctor had noticed something unusual with her heartbeat at her sixth-month visit. He held the stethoscope to my ear and said, "You hear that? That soft murmur?" he asked.

I put the ear pieces in and listened. There was a distinct but faint *whoosh* accompanying Maddie's heartbeat. He put the end of the stethoscope on Emma's chest, and I listened to hers. Only a strong, solid beating could be heard in her chubby chest as she grabbed the end of the stethoscope and tried to chew on it.

"I am pretty sure Maddie has a hole in her heart," he said.

The technical term we'd learn was atrial septal defect (ASD). A "hole" in the wall separated the top two chambers of Maddie's heart. Babies are born with this opening, and it is supposed to close within weeks or months after birth. If it remains open and is small, it won't cause symptoms. But the larger the hole, the harder the heart and lungs have to work to repump blood that is flowing the wrong way.

"Maddie is basically running a marathon sitting still," he explained.

A consult with a cardiologist confirmed our pediatrician's diagnosis. "I'm afraid she is going to need open-heart surgery." Maddie was nine months old.

While open-heart surgery sounded terrifying to Charlie and me, the doctors were confident in this routine cardiac surgery, calling it the "appendectomy of the heart world." But the fact was, they would be opening the chest of our tiny baby girl, stopping her heart, making the repair, and closing her back up.

Maddie would have two scars—one the entire length of her chest and a smaller one from the drainage tubes. She could live with the scars, but I wasn't sure how I could live without Maddie. If this didn't go well, how could I ever look at Emma and not think of her other half? How does any mother survive the loss of a child?

In the weeks leading up to the surgery, I worried incessantly.

"You might try some prayer," Dad suggested on the phone.

"I wish I thought that would work, Dad, but I don't," I told him.

"I know. I wish you did too," he said. "I'll try some for you."

"Thanks, Dad," I said. "I'm just not sure God listens."

"You'll see someday," he said. "You may not think he does, but I absolutely believe it's true. God might not send you exactly what you expect, but he's always with you."

God must have heard Dad because Maddie's surgery was

successful. By day three she was sitting up eating pancakes with her fingers, and on day four she was discharged. As a toddler, Maddie would proudly point to her tummy and call her scar her "stripe." Her energy level continued to be exuberant as well, so Charlie nicknamed her Tigger. Three months after her open-heart surgery, we celebrated Maddie and Emma's first birthday. Our family of six was whole once again. Our four girls squished together in the kitchen as I brought out a zebra cake, Charlie's favorite, made with thin chocolate cookies covered in whipped cream and refrigerated into gooey goodness. The twins wriggled and giggled, unable to blow out their candles, so Lauren and Kailey did it for them while the younger sisters watched wide-eyed.

No one needed to make a wish; so many had already come true.

six

SOUP AND SALVATION

Here is my secret. It's quite simple: One sees clearly only
with the heart. Anything essential is invisible to the eyes.

—Antoine de Saint-Exupéry[1]

Being a mom myself and seeing how difficult it was to respond to
all the needs and emotions of girls began to soften the stone in my
heart toward my own mother. It was humbling to realize just how
difficult it was to be a mom with a working, albeit sleep-deprived,
brain, much less one battling depression and mania.

I thought about how my parents had worked to do things in
the community even while raising three daughters and struggling
with Mom's chronic illness. Throughout it all Dad had volunteered,
served in the church, and run his legal practice.

Charlie worked as an investment wealth manager, so he worried
constantly about how we would afford four kids and how we could
plan for their futures. I worried constantly about how we would

raise four good kids. How I would teach the two commandments I learned from my family: Do Good, and Love Well.

Church was not a place I wanted to revisit with our girls. All those hours spent trying to sit still in the pew were merely the price I had to pay to be rewarded at Gigi's dinner table. I never felt like the sermons were meant for me and certainly did not believe church had molded any part of my character. Now that I had a choice, I was not going to force religion on our daughters. Charlie and I felt in control of our own fate, working hard to be self-reliant to get what we needed.

No outside prayers required.

But Charlotte is a city where it is easier to opt in to religion than to opt out. Charlotte is sometimes called "The City of Churches" because a house of faith is on nearly every corner. Even today most stores open only after 1:00 p.m. on Sundays because sales are too slow until churches let out.

The most Christian thing our family did on Sundays was go swimming at the YMCA indoor pool.

One day while juggling four towels and the twins' floaties, our little wet herd was leaving the Y when Lauren stopped to study a framed portrait by the front door. She asked earnestly, "Mommy, who's that man?"

It was Jesus.

My parents and grandparents would have been horrified to hear her question. In an effort to ensure our daughters could at least name this iconic biblical figure, we began attending a church: First Presbyterian Church of Charlotte.

We'd been going only a few months when I was reminded of one reason I had abandoned organized religion—getting dressed. My mom would have had my daughters decked out with perfectly combed hair tied with ribbons, matching smocked dresses, and tights with no holes.

I was struggling to get my four daughters into shoes. Inevitably, by the time I had wrestled all four into their Sunday best, there wasn't a sermon anywhere that could save me from this weekly fashion exhaustion.

But a small ad in the church bulletin offered divine inspiration:

Volunteers needed for the First Presbyterian soup kitchen team!
Every fourth Sunday morning, all ages welcome!
Contact the Volunteer Coordinator Office.

Finally a place where we could do good and not have to look good. I signed up our family to work one Sunday a month from 8:00 a.m. to 1:00 p.m. The volunteer coordinator told me we would be helping at Charlotte's Urban Ministry Center (UMC), which served the homeless. Our duties would include preparing soup in the thirty-gallon pot, making hundreds of sandwiches, and then serving lunch.

We piled into the minivan that first Sunday and followed the directions to the ministry center. As we turned off the interstate, we saw a hundred yards of street ahead leading directly into a chain-link fence. There was no building that we could see, just dozens of people standing, sitting, even sleeping on the sidewalk. As we pulled closer, we could see signage on an old train depot that had been converted to the city's outreach center for the homeless.

The UMC opened its gates in the parking lot at 8:00 a.m., but dozens of people lugging possessions on their backs were already waiting to be let inside. Faces were hidden under gray hoods, and their ages and genders were impossible to tell.

"Are you sure this is a good idea?" Charlie asked.

In answering the ad in the church bulletin, I had expected a feel-good family-volunteer opportunity. The girls had never seen extreme poverty so up close and personal. Charlie pulled the car forward slowly so as not to hit one of the many bodies spilling over the sidewalks. I was nervous. It felt mildly dangerous and reckless to be bringing our girls here.

An effusive woman with frosted gray hair and red lips met us at the front door of the depot.

"Hey! Y'all must be the Izard family!" she gushed. "I am Beverly, and this is my husband, Roy!" I recognized them from the few times we had been at First Presbyterian Church.

We all relaxed a little. Beverly led us into the kitchen where a thirty-gallon soup pot was already simmering with a vegetable stew. Roy wore an apron and was gently stirring a lumpy, bubbling liquid.

"So what kind is it?" Kailey asked him.

"All kinds!" he said brightly. "Ever heard of the story *Stone Soup*? It's like that. We put in a little bit of everything!"

We would be serving lunch for anywhere between four and six hundred people. This happened 365 days a year, all food made and served by volunteers. The UMC never missed a day. Over the years there had been ice storms, power outages, even a blizzard or two, but the center was always open from 8:30 to 4:30 every day.

Homeless people don't get holidays off, and neither did the center.

During the weekdays, more volunteers came to help provide services beyond lunch: counseling, showers, laundry, mail. Beverly let us know that our day, the fourth Sunday of the month, was one of the biggest days for lunch crowds because it was at the end of the month when food stamps and incomes ran short.

Promptly at 11:30, Roy rolled up the steel window cover over the six-foot-long counter separating the dining room from the kitchen. "Come on, girls, let's go welcome our guests," he said. "Now everyone who comes today is going to get served no questions asked. And we call everyone Neighbor, just like your neighbor at home."

All four girls scooted after him to unlock the door. Roy stood out in the parking lot next to the line and shook hands with a couple of the regulars he recognized. Roy called out down the line, "Y'all bow your heads, and we will say a little blessing."

Lauren, Kailey, Emma, and Maddie stood close to his side as he prayed.

"Dear Lord, bless this food to our use and us to thy service, and make us ever mindful of the needs of others. Amen."

A chorus of amens rippled down the line.

As the line started to move through, few spoke but almost all nodded a thank-you. One of the few who tried to engage us was a wild-eyed gentleman who called out, "Hey, pretty girls, how are you?"

He had matted white hair, a sunburned face, and a Harley-Davidson logo tattooed on the middle of his forehead. He balanced a small boom box, more of a radio really, in one hand as he took his tray with the other.

Lauren and Kailey stared at him. "Hi. Have a nice day," Kailey eeked out.

"You know what my name is, darlin'?" he asked them.

"Harley?" Kailey guessed.

"Nope! It's Chilly. Chilly Willy! Cuz I'm a cool guy! The coolest there is! The coolest you'll ever meet!"

By now he had all my girls' attention as Maddie and Emma ran over to get a closer look. Now that he had a bigger audience, Chilly Willy started hamming it up with a particularly bad rendition of Charlie Daniels Band's "Long Haired Country Boy," about getting stoned in the morning and drunk in the afternoon.

"Thank you, Chilly," a man interrupted. He had graying hair and a gray mustache, making him look older, but I guessed he was in his late forties. He wore glasses with thick black frames that gave him a serious look, but he joked easily with Chilly Willy. "Let's save the Grand Ole Opry for another time. We have a line of people here who want to get their lunch."

"Hey, Dale!" Chilly gave the man a huge hug and turned to my girls. "This here's the boss man. I got to do what he says. He's a preacher too. Jesus loves you, Dale!"

"He loves you, too, Chilly; now eat that lunch," Dale said, as he patted Chilly gently on the back to send him on his way.

As our family worked to serve the Neighbors their lunch, we were introduced to Dale Mullennix. Dale had been the executive director of the Urban Ministry Center since the day it opened. He had been a minister at a wealthy suburban church in an affluent section of town where we lived until he was asked to take on this job in the early 1990s. Business and faith leaders were working to make the UMC a full-service center for the homeless, not just a kitchen open at lunch. This new mission in the renovated train depot needed a director, and Dale was asked to be the first leader.

"Thank you all for coming out today!" he said to us, shaking each of our hands. Dale then moved into the dining room, going table to table and greeting most everyone by name.

"Hey, Rose, how you doing today? Sam, how's the foot?" Dale said. He handed out hugs and handshakes like everyone was a good friend. I had spent the past few hours safely behind the stainless-steel lunch counter afraid to make eye contact with anyone.

What if someone asked me for money? Should I give it to them? How did Dale go home and not want to take everyone with him?

Finally it was time to clean up, and the girls were giddy. "That was so fun, Mom!" Lauren said.

"Can we come back tomorrow?" Kailey asked.

In the car on the way home there were more questions.

"Mom, can a food stamp mail a letter too?"

"Dad, how can a man have a gold chain but no house?"

"Why did that nice lady have a black eye and no front teeth?"

I had grown up familiar with the income disparity between El Paso and Juarez, but here in Charlotte, I had become much more insulated from poverty. That first visit to the soup kitchen triggered my slow realization that less than three miles from my comfortable Charlotte home was another world.

Month after month, my education evolved. Eventually I took Beverly's job and became the Fourth Sunday Soup Kitchen Captain for the church, recruiting our daughters' friends and families to join us. Mostly I stayed safely behind the kitchen counter, but I came to know the names of some regulars. Ruth was the tiny, surly woman who, despite her size, seemed to rule huge men with her biting tongue. Staff told me Ruth had been at the UMC on the day it opened and had come every day since. Jay was the incredibly loud drunk who was wildly disruptive when he had too many beers but unrecognizably sweet when sober. Bill was the quiet cowboy with huge blue eyes under a leather hat who always said, "Please" and "Thank you, ma'am" when handed his tray. And Samuel was the gentle giant with the smile of a seven-year-old boy on Christmas morning just about any time you even looked his direction.

Though I'd never found religion in a pew, each Sunday in the soup kitchen made me feel a little more like someone I wanted to be. Each month at the end of our shift, I could take off my apron, hug my girls, drive out the gates, and feel I had done a little good in the world.

For a long time that was enough.

—

It wasn't until our den ceiling started to leak that homelessness inched a little closer to my home. I called our plumber, Johnny, who had been working for us ever since he had replumbed the entire house Charlie and I bought as newlyweds. Johnny had been upstairs all morning looking for the source of the water dripping onto our hardwood floor below. He came into the kitchen before lunch and apologized. "I need to go meet my brother at Freedom Park and give him some money."

"Just tell him to come here," I offered.

"You don't understand," he said, dropping his gaze to the floor and shifting his feet uncomfortably. "My brother lives in the park."

He was right. I didn't understand. Freedom Park was less than half a mile from our house, and we went there all the time for the girls' soccer games or to ride bikes. His brother lived there? Did Johnny mean in a nearby house?

He saw my confusion and clarified with visible shame. "He's homeless."

Johnny tried to explain the unexplainable.

"My brother did something bad when he was seventeen and went to prison. When he got out, he was never quite right. Nothing seems to help, but he calls me when he needs something, like his radio . . ."

"Radio?" With that clue, I connected the dots. "Johnny, is your brother that guy with the white hair and tattoo on his forehead? Chilly Willy?"

Johnny nodded, cringing at the street name. "His real name is Larry. William Larry Major. He's my brother."

I had no idea what to say. All those times serving soup, I had never thought about the families of the homeless.

"I worry he's going to die out there and we won't know," Johnny confessed.

Since that very first meeting when I had served Chilly Willy soup, I never thought that he had a given name: Larry. I never thought about who his family was or how he ended up in a soup kitchen, a twenty-four-inch-wide stainless-steel counter between us. Me on the right side, Chilly Willy on the wrong side.

"Everybody in town knows him, and when they don't see him for a while, they call and ask me if he's dead. I have to call the police stations and hospitals to find out if he's still alive," Johnny admitted, tearing up.

I couldn't say anything to help Johnny, but I started looking for Chilly Willy when I was at the park and at the UMC, just so I could tell Johnny I had seen his brother very much alive.

Chilly Willy was William Larry Major.

He had a brother, a family, and a story behind how he had ended up on the streets of Charlotte.

And like my mother, Larry had people who loved him and worried about him all the time.

seven

FAILURE IS NOT AN OPTION

It's not hard to decide what you want your life to be about.
What's hard, she said, is figuring out what you're willing to
give up in order to do the things you really care about.

—Shauna Niequist[1]

I decided early on in my life that failure was not an option. If I couldn't succeed pretty quickly at something I tried, I usually threw in the towel at the first moment failure emerged as a possibility.

I generally felt there were two reasons to quit. One: failure was probable, like piano playing. My sister Allyson had innate, unfathomable talent that I couldn't possibly measure up to, so I begged my mom to let me quit Mrs. Wade's piano school after only two years. The second reason I felt it was acceptable to quit was if the work needed to attain success was not fun. This is why my tennis career ended.

Dad was not a gifted athlete when he was young. In Texas,

football was the only real sport for boys, but Dad was too small to be a star player. Gigi and Poppa wanted to find something he could excel at beyond the classroom, and they found it on the tennis court. Dad practiced religiously, realizing this was his avenue not only to avoid being teased at school but also to gain entrance eventually to the prestigious Davidson College. Dad loved the game and wanted his three daughters to love it too.

Teaching us tennis began as his way of giving Mom a break on the weekends after he'd kept long work hours during the week. But Dad also used his expertise at tennis to impart his wisdom to us.

Every Saturday morning Dad had a standing doubles game with the same guys at the El Paso Tennis Club. On Saturday afternoon he would come home to play tennis with his three girls. He kept an overflowing hopper of tennis balls in the trunk of his blue Ford El Torino, and we'd drive to the public tennis courts where he'd patiently hit to each of us.

As it became apparent that I had been blessed with the best hand-eye coordination of the Green Girls, these group outings thinned as first Louise and then Allyson dropped out. Saturdays became my father-daughter time, and I treasured the weekly one-on-one attention.

"Everything in life is about hard work, Kathy! Hard work and practice!" he would yell across the net as he fed me balls. This was his chance to mold both my game and my character.

Though I never tired of the time with my dad, my love of tennis began to wane—it was just too difficult for me to become really good at it.

I had stuck with tennis because I was reasonably proficient and because it gave my dad so much pleasure. But to win tournaments, I realized, was going to take a lot of work.

At my father's insistence I entered the citywide under-thirteen girls' doubles competition with my friend Susan. Her father worked at the same law firm as my dad, and they loved to compare notes on their daughters' swings and stats. Much to my surprise, but not to my father's, Susan and I won. Instead of trophies we were each given small silver medals, and our names were printed in the newspaper the next day.

"I told you! I told you!" he exclaimed, grabbing me in a bear hug that lasted a full minute. "You can do anything, Kathy! Really, anything!"

His smile lasted through breakfast and beyond.

"We can start playing on Sundays after church before you go back for youth group. I can get the club pro to give you some lessons too. I think he can help your serve."

It took almost a full year of those extra lessons before I worked up the courage to quit. The disappointment was crushing for Dad, but I couldn't take any more. I had reached the point where I knew the work needed to attain success was not fun. I now hated tennis.

Dad was sitting at his desk in the den when I got up the nerve to tell him. To his right were the bookshelves that held some of his favorite tennis trophies and lifetime achievement awards. My heart was in my throat as I approached with the precious medal that meant so much to him. I reached for his hand, pressing it into his palm.

"Dad, you are right; maybe I could do it," I confessed. "I'm sorry I just don't want to."

It would be twenty-five years before I picked up a tennis racquet again.

I could feel his disappointment in me every Saturday when he'd come home from his men's doubles game at the tennis club. Instead of rushing inside for me and heading to the park with his hopper of balls, he'd sit heavily on the den couch.

Without the excuse to take me to play, we stayed in the house on Saturdays. He'd hint around the edges of conversation, but he never had been good at small talk with us. Without that court full of sunshine, he didn't know how to teach life lessons.

I know there was so much he needed to tell me and so much we should have been talking about. But back in that house that held all our secrets and sadness, Dad just couldn't find the words.

———

I didn't realize how important that time with my dad was until I was in my forties. It was 1997, and it was supposed to be a very good year.

The twins were turning three. Maddie's scars from her heart surgery had healed, and I thought medical worries were behind us.

I was stirring a big pot of meat sauce for spaghetti when the phone rang. Emma was at my feet chewing on the Tupperware cup that had held her Cheerios, which were now spread across the hardwood floor. I could hear Maddie pretending she was in a race car zooming from kitchen to den to living room.

My Buddha Baby and my Tasmanian Devil.

The phone shrilled insistently. Carefully stepping over Emma, I reached for the receiver.

"Hey, it's Dad," he said. I checked my watch. My dad never called this early.

"Is it Mom? Is she okay?"

"Actually, it's me, Kathy. I have cancer."

I struggled to think. I readily absorbed bad news about my mom. We all worried about my mom. We had experience with that. I had no idea how to process this.

"What kind, Dad? Is it bad?"

"It's leukemia—acute myeloid leukemia. We are going to MD

Anderson in Houston. Their doctors are the best, and you know me—I will fight this!"

He left off the "and win!" but I supposed it went without saying that he believed he would.

He always won. He worked hard. He practiced. He never gave up. Winning was the natural, logical outcome to perseverance.

I hung up the phone, shattered.

Word of Dad's diagnosis spread quickly—El Paso is basically a small town. Unlike my mom's illness, everyone talked about Dad's cancer. The Presbyterians and all my parents' friends showed up strong.

Cards. Casseroles. Compassion. We were inundated.

Dad and Mom spent nine months in Houston so he could receive an experimental treatment that we learned was his only option. Trial therapy doctors told us they would take his blood marrow cells down to zero and build them back up again with the hope that the new marrow would not have the cancer cells. Dad lived in a sterile environment at MD Anderson, and my mom lived in the hotel attached to the cancer center.

Dad's new home was a twelve-by-twelve-foot room with a hospital bed. He was confined there twenty-four hours a day connected to tubes on rolling IV poles he could push around his cell of hope. A five-foot glass window on one wall allowed him to see visitors and my mom. She was his constant companion on the other side of the glass, reading and needlepointing.

Our girls made cards for "Poppy" and "Lili" that Mom taped to his window on the world. Dad would proudly point to the artwork, telling the nurses about each of his four granddaughters.

His room had no natural light and no way to escape to a tennis court, so Dad asked hospital staff to bring an exercise bike into his solitary confinement. He would pedal furiously while watching tennis tournaments and wearing a T-shirt that proclaimed "Never, never give up!" It was given to him by a cancer survivor.

Louise, Allyson, and I rotated weeks visiting our parents in Houston. While I had been to visit Mom on psychiatric wards, I was unprepared for the distinct difference on cancer wards. So much of the disease of the mind happens on the inside with so much invisible to the eye. With cancer and disease of the body, so much was plainly visible. Weight loss. Hair loss. Hollow eyes. Gaunt skin. There was no question who were the patients and who were the caregivers. But in both cancer and mental illness, I learned, families' hopes held on to pills and protocols that took far too long to reverse the course of suffering.

I always worried I would arrive on one of those visits to Houston to find Mom battling extreme depression or mania. Yet during those agonizing months, she was the strongest, best version of herself. The one who had dazzled in college, planned my gorgeous wedding, and created old-fashioned paper dolls for her granddaughters. Dad needed her in this medical crisis, and Mom was steady and fully present. She seemed to summon an uncommon strength to be there for him as he had always been there for her. Mom became an expert in AML blast cells and CBC counts, always a calm but insistent advocate when a nurse was late with pain medication.

Witnessing this new side of my mother meant in some strange way that I enjoyed those visits to Houston. It may have been the first time in decades we really had a conversation. Mom and I would go to dinner each night, escaping the medical compound in search of chile con queso (for me) and a good crab cake (for her). We found ways to distract ourselves from the ever-present worry, but the conversation usually circled back to Dad and God.

"Are you worried?" I'd ask.

"Your dad and I have a strong faith," she'd answer, which did not really answer the question.

Each day my parents waited, prayed, and read the Bible just like on their first Valentine's Day date.

Faith, hope, and love abide.

At the end of that first trial, the doctors told my parents that research indicated 60 percent of patients responded to treatment. My dad was not one of them.

The oncologists told Dad he could repeat the treatment. More living in Houston. More tubes. More weeks in the glass bubble. In the second round of treatment, research showed that nearly 80 percent of the unlucky 40 percent who did not see results in the first trial would achieve success in the second round. My dad was not one of them.

He went home to El Paso, a little more shaken in his belief that a medical miracle might occur. Since he had worked so diligently all his life for his law firm, for the church, for the community, he had delayed time for himself. Cancer had arrived unexpectedly with his retirement package. Dad would not concede that it was possible all his plans to see the world might not happen. The train trip across Europe might never leave the station. Doctors advised him to save his strength, but he kept playing tennis with his regular Saturday foursome; only he didn't run for every ball. When doctors said it would be impossible to get on a plane to New York for Allyson's wedding because his white blood cell count was too low, he stubbornly walked the bride down the aisle anyway.

Over the years I had imagined many times what it would be like to lose my mom. But I had never imagined losing my father. While my mother had always been somewhat of a question mark in my life, Dad was the exclamation point. He was solid and steady. He anchored me and our family. He encouraged me, believed in me, and dreamed for me dreams I didn't even have for myself.

Although I didn't want to think about it, Dad began to make

plans for that eventuality. I was the youngest daughter, and he let me know he was leaving me in charge not only as executor of his estate but also of all of Mom's ongoing legal and financial affairs. Even though I had never gone to law school, Dad said he trusted my logical mind and Charlie's financial savvy to handle whatever eventualities might arise. Just as he had for his clients, Dad planned everything meticulously. He created a five-page document with every account, investment, and obligation listed with his specific wishes spelled out. One afternoon when I phoned to check on him, he said he was writing his obituary.

"Dad! Stop! That's morbid!" I told him.

"No, it's not! I'm just at the good part about the loving wife and three daughters!"

Even as he carefully planned for the end, I think he had a secret hope that the illness was a test of his faith. Maybe if he just believed and prayed enough, there would be a miracle cure.

As he grew weaker, Dad's anger flashed.

He had lived a good life. He had been a good servant. Why was this happening?

He wouldn't yell at God, but he could yell at Mom.

She didn't yell back—at God or Dad. Whatever she was thinking, she kept to herself and remained resolutely loving and soothing.

But the greatest of these is love.

I did not share my father's hope that God would intervene. But I was unreasonably hopeful for Dad's recovery because his resilience and optimism convinced me he had years ahead of him still.

He didn't look sick. He still played tennis. There was no way he could die.

Still hopeful, I met my parents at Dad's favorite beachside resort in La Jolla, California, where my family had rented a home during several summers when I was growing up. I spent that week with him and my mom revisiting our favorite places. By then I had taken up playing tennis again, and Dad challenged me to a match. Even in his weakened state, he easily won both sets. Dad still had a mean drop shot. Throughout our match he grinned mischievously as he forced me to chase balls on the baseline before sending a wily short shot for a winner.

I wish I had used that trip, that court time, to say more. With the court between us full of sunshine, I wish I had called joyously across to him, "You are the best, Dad!"

On the changeovers as we sipped water, I should have whispered, "You have always been here for me, Dad. No matter what happened to Mom, I always knew you'd never leave me alone."

And when he won that last set, I wish I had jumped across the net and given him a bear hug and a victory grin that would have lasted through breakfast and beyond.

We didn't say all that we could have. We talked about ways to improve my forehand or his remarkable drop shot. We acted as if there would always be another match, another game.

Six weeks later, not even a year after his first symptoms began, I called to check on him on a Saturday morning, and he admitted he wasn't feeling well.

"Are you going to call your doctor?" I asked.

"No, I'm sure it is just the hot dog I ate at the UT El Paso basketball game last night," he said, before adding, "It won't kill me."

My dad, John Leighton Green Jr., died that night, November 15, 1998, at sixty-four.

It had been only ten months and ten days since we were introduced to leukemia. I may have been thirty-five, but with my father gone I felt abandoned. Until then, in every sandstorm, Dad had always been on the other end of the rope steadfastly holding tight.

I had many months to contemplate this, to prepare for this

moment. I guess that is the small consolation with cancer. You have time to begin to say what should have been said and make up for all the moments that will be stolen from you.

I gathered my girls to tell them. Lauren was eight, Kailey six, Emma and Maddie, four.

"You all know Poppy has been sick and that he has been in the hospital a lot." I couldn't keep my voice from cracking. Lauren didn't know what I was trying to tell her, but she knew it wasn't good.

"But he's going to be okay, right, Mom?"

There was no lying on this one, no making it better, no softening it. As much as I never wanted my girls to be sad or hurt, there was no fixing this. I touched her blond head and started crying. "No, honey, I'm sorry. He won't be okay. Poppy died last night."

I'm not sure Kailey, Emma, and Maddie fully grasped the situation, but they knew if Lauren was crying, they should be crying too.

Laurenkaileyemmamaddie. One body, four hearts.

Emma must have been thinking about her other grandfather's garden overflowing with vegetables in Rye. Tagging behind Charlie's dad, the girls had all seen vegetable plants alive and abundant in the summer become lifeless, dormant stalks in the winter. The next summer those same dead plants would once again be magically resurrected with the weight of new growth. "Mommy, Poppy will grow back—right?" Emma had asked.

For his birthday four months earlier, I had given Dad a brown leather journal, and on the front I had embossed the words *Poppy Talk*.

Dad was going to write his story and impart all the wisdom he wanted his granddaughters to know.

Mom told me that on his last night in the hospital, Dad had instructed the nurse to put the IV in his left arm to make sure he could use his right arm to write. He had more stories to tell. More he needed to say.

There was so much Dad had tried to tell me, too, that I could not hear. I wanted to listen now. I wanted to play tennis with him now. I was ready to play the game now. I wanted him to see that I could work hard at something and never, never give up.

You can do anything, Kathy, really, anything.

He had imagined the unimaginable for me. The only way I could ever feel surrounded by his love again was to prove him right.

eight

WORKING MY WAY HOME

Whatever we choose, however we decide to use our days,
the shape of our days becomes the shape of our lives.

—Wayne Muller[1]

You can do anything, Kathy, really, anything. The thought haunted me after Dad died.

What could I do that mattered?

At thirty-five I was an accidental tourist in my own life. I had built the family I had craved and a career I reasonably enjoyed, but as far as any dreams, I had none. Somewhere between the three pregnancies and the baby weight that had never gone away, I had become sedentary, just watching my life from the safety of my couch.

My father's death dislodged my complacency. Something inside began to stir, urging me to think differently. I was not willing anymore to let my life happen to me. I needed to do something, risk something, but I felt stuck.

One week during a third-grade after-school meeting for Kailey's class, I overheard one of the moms, Sarah Belk, talking to her friends. "I am going on a weeklong horse pack trip in the Wind River Range with three of my kids! We will be riding horses and sleeping in the wilderness in teepees!"

I loved horses but had not ridden since summer camp when I was in third grade. I had never camped in the wilderness.

"You should come!" Sarah's face lit up as she spoke to me. Her brown eyes were inviting, and her hand gestures welcoming. "It's going to be so fun and even better if our girls can hang together!"

That was how I found myself riding horses up a mountainside with Lauren and Kailey in the summer of 1999. Charlie stayed home watching the twins. Sarah was riding ahead with three of her five children following our leaders, a married couple, Abie and Grant Beck of Pinedale, Wyoming. Although we were roughly the same age, Abie had a long blond ponytail swinging out of her baseball cap, bulging biceps, and slim Levi's that would have never fit my thighs. That morning she had expertly packed eleven horses and two mules while Grant sipped his coffee and smoked cigarettes over a campfire. Abie was now fearlessly leading us nine thousand feet into the completely untouched Bridger Wilderness.

"Isn't this awesome?" Sarah gushed, looking back over her shoulder at me. "I am so glad you all came!"

I tried to give her an equally enthusiastic grin, but my knees were already screaming at me, and I seemed to have no muscle memory of saddles from third-grade summer camp. We were making our way to the highest point of our trip, which Abie lovingly referred to as "Grant's Peak."

Looking nervously at the peak, I wasn't sure I could make it because it looked like something out of *The Sound of Music* only with more boulders. It took us all morning to reach the base, and now we were dismounting to summit on foot.

"Oh, Lordy," Sarah said—her favorite southern expression coming out as we sweated, climbing over each gray obstacle.

It was a steady uphill climb made easier at times by giant rocks that formed a virtual staircase to the top. Just short of the peak we encountered a vast snowfield. Our kids, dressed only in their T-shirts and jeans, slid across it, pretending to snowboard in their cowboy boots. Clouds were gathering, so we hurried to the "Top of the World," as Abie called it. We cheered as we made the summit, Sarah and I high-fiving and our kids gathered around us taking photos of the triumph.

The day had started out a beautiful seventy degrees, but now the clouds were thick and angry looking. We scrambled down trying to beat the storm and the thirty-degree temperature drop. Booming thunder rocked the sky as hail began to pop around us. As we pulled thin raincoats over the T-shirts and jeans, realization set in. We were a two-and-a-half-hour wet horseback ride from our camp, and this storm was not stopping.

During the next two hours, I fantasized about a lot of things. A truck to come pick us up. A lodge to rise up in the distance. A longer raincoat. None of them magically appeared.

An hour into the misery, Kailey turned in her saddle to look back at me and wail, "I'm so cold, Mom, I can't go anymore."

Fearing mutiny from all the kids if one buckled, I channeled an inner-general voice I didn't know I had. "You will, Kailey. We all will because we have no choice."

Kailey looked stunned not to receive a more motherly rescue solution. She whipped around in her saddle and hunkered into a silent wet lump for the rest of the ride.

When we finally sloshed into camp, all our kids were so frozen in their saddles we had to help them off their horses. We ducked into our teepee, peeling off soaking jeans, and I zipped Lauren and Kailey shivering into their sleeping bags. I tried to think how I would entertain them without leaving the six-foot shelter for the rest of the night.

"Have Dad and I ever taught you to play poker?"

By the light of our battery lantern, we played Texas Hold'em as we belted out all the words we could remember to our favorite Dixie Chicks and Shania Twain songs. We finished the evening with a rousing round of "Man, I Feel Like a Woman."

The funny thing is, I really did finally feel like a woman. A strong, capable, I-can-do-anything woman. We salvaged that day, that night, and then the whole trip. I did things I never thought I could do and used muscles I had forgotten I possessed.

This trip was exactly as I had hoped. I'd never be the same.

I had heard Dale Mullennix speak once at the Urban Ministry Center about serving the homeless. Dale said one of his volunteers told him he was "ruined for life" after working there because he could never look at a plate of food the same way again. Having witnessed at the UMC the reality of having nothing, he would always be incredibly grateful for everything.

After that week in the Wind River Range, I felt the same. I'd never look at my bed the same way again. Or my shower or a rainstorm. All week it had taken so little to be happy. A campfire. A sunny day. Chocolate in my trail mix at lunch. And I knew that when I looked at Lauren and Kailey, I would now know they could handle anything.

I was ruined for life and grateful for it.

Charlie met us in the airport at the baggage claim. When our duffle came up, I instinctively stepped in front of him and hoisted it easily off the belt as I had been doing all week.

"Whoa!" he said laughing. "What happened out there?"

"I think I found myself," I answered.

"I didn't know you were lost."

"I truly didn't either."

———

That trip created a new restlessness inside me, and I vowed I was not going to sleepwalk through my life anymore. I wanted to quit my graphic-design job, but economically that was hard to justify. I had a great business with good clients who paid me well and a home office where I set my own schedule. But I was no longer happy being just Graphics Girl. I wanted to do something that mattered.

Almost nine years would go by as I wrestled with what I wanted to be when I grew up. I considered graduate school, but that seemed impossible with children. Besides, I had no idea what I would study. I wandered the aisles of bookstores looking for books on career change that might have the magic answer to my midlife misery.

How would I know what I was meant to do? I kept waiting for that aha moment, like the one when I met Charlie and knew he was the one. My moment of purpose would surely present itself to me now that I was searching for it.

I kept busy with work and volunteering while I waited for my life to find me. I joined the boards of several organizations in Charlotte and tried helping nonprofits with good causes: education, mentoring, and even an orphanage in Africa. My life was busy but not full.

I was still in search mode when my horseback buddy Sarah and her husband, Tim, invited us to attend a "Forty Years of Service" fundraiser for Outward Bound. The evening was a tribute to one volunteer, Rufus Dalton, who had left an indelible mark on the organization by his sustained dedication to their mission for over four decades. His singlemindedness made me think about all my scattershot efforts in the past few years. Maybe that was the reason I hadn't found something that mattered—I had never stayed with one thing long enough.

As we drove home, Charlie asked, "So what would your forty-year thing be?"

I didn't have any idea. For almost twenty years I had been able to study a problem and distill it down to a single, simple solution for my clients. A logo. A headline. A tagline.

But now I was the client. I needed an idea. And I could not think of a single one. Not one thing I felt capable of accomplishing that would matter in this world.

Where was the big idea for my life?

———

In February 2007, it arrived. And I never saw it coming.

I started reading a book Mom had recently told me about: *Same Kind of Different As Me* by Ron Hall and Denver Moore. Honestly, I picked it up only to give me something, besides retirement homes, to talk about with my mom. We had started the dreaded family conversation about Mom's selling her house and downsizing.

The book grabbed me from the beginning and never let go.

The story tells how Ron Hall went to the Fort Worth Union Gospel Mission after cheating on his wife, Debbie, because he thought that following her passion to the soup kitchen would be a way to make amends. But once there Ron allowed himself to truly know and care for one person—Denver Moore.

"You is blessin' folks with your dollars and service," Ron used to hear Denver say, "but a dollar bill and plate of food ain't changin' a life."

As crazy as it might seem, Ron and Debbie invited Denver—who had been thirty years homeless—to come into their home, their lives, and after that nothing was the same.

I had been serving soup with a smile for years, but how many people was I truly helping? How many people did I really know?

I finished the book, but it wouldn't leave me. In fact, it haunted me. Ron and Debbie had done something—they ended one person's homelessness. For all my service at the soup kitchen, I had never done anything even close to that. The book sat on my bedside table, and every time I saw the cover, I heard the strangest thought whispering over and over: *invite them to Charlotte.*

A few days after finishing the book, I composed an e-mail to Ron, introducing myself as a board member of the Urban Ministry Center (true) and asked if he would consider coming to North Carolina for a planned fundraiser (false).

I pressed send and immediately regretted it.

Full of guilt, I stared at the key that had launched my lie into cyberspace. I hoped Ron didn't read e-mails or, if he did, he would delete mine.

Twenty minutes later a reply from Ron blinked in my in-box:

Yes, we do accept speaking engagements. When is your event?

I could feel perspiration begin to form as I typed a complete lie:

I need to get with my committee, but hold the second week in November.

The next day I sheepishly walked into Dale Mullennix's office with a copy of Ron and Denver's book to confess I had accidently booked a speaker for a fundraiser we had not planned. After some small talk I started bumbling through an explanation of *Same Kind of Different As Me*, noting what a huge following it had in Texas. I tried to interject some spiritual references, mentioning the book was in some weird way calling to me.

Neither of us was sure what we were agreeing to, but I left his office with a skeptical yes: I would plan a "friendraiser" around Ron and Denver's visit to help raise awareness for the UMC.

A few days later I gathered with three friends, including Sarah, in a restaurant booth to celebrate Angela Breeden's birthday. I explained to them what had happened when I e-mailed Ron.

"Ooh, Kathy, this sounds like a great book and a great idea!" Sarah said, even though she had never heard of *Same Kind of Different As Me*.

Everyone at the table agreed and was caught up in the infectious excitement. "I'll run the bank!" Angela offered.

"I'll host a party for Ron and Denver!" said Kim, Sarah's sister-in-law.

"We can order a bunch of copies and give them to our friends to start firing people up!" Sarah said.

No one at the table had ever orchestrated something like this, but we had all helped with church and school events. We felt that together we might be able to pull it off.

We set the date for Thursday, November 14, 2007, and since it was approaching Thanksgiving, we brainstormed a title for our luncheon: True Blessings. The idea was to create an inspiring event before the holidays with a *true* message about homelessness from Ron and Denver. We wouldn't charge anyone to come. We hoped the day would be so moving that friends would write checks to help cover the cost of food and the expenses of getting the famous authors here from Texas.

I felt terrified but exhilarated. I couldn't see how any of this was going to turn out, but it also felt like I was going in the right direction for the first time in a long while.

nine

GOING FOR A RIDE

The only important thing in a book is
the meaning that it has for you.

—W. Somerset Maugham[1]

I picked up Ron and Denver on Wednesday, November 13, 2007, at the Charlotte airport, trying to appear confident. Our little group of moms had been overly successful, and the planned small event for one hundred guests at church had mushroomed into over one thousand people who wanted to come support the homeless. We had moved the event twice to accommodate the expanding crowd and finally booked Charlotte's largest ballroom. The past few months I had lost a lot of sleep wondering why I had ever listened to that whisper to invite Ron and Denver to Charlotte.

When the dynamic duo got into my car, however, they were not exactly living up to their press. The pair billed as having an amazing and "unlikely friendship" arrived for our event in a silent feud. In the car on the way to lunch, Ron explained the rift.

A couple of nights before, they were honored guests at a fund-raising dinner in Texas. Former first lady Barbara Bush had read their book and invited them to "A Celebration of Reading" promoting literacy.

News of this high-profile engagement shocked me. I had no idea they were in such demand when I sent my e-mail six months before. Ron laughed, telling me Denver's famous quote about the Texas event: "I done gone from livin' in the bushes to eatin' with the Bushes. God bless America, this is a great country!"

Although Denver had now been off the streets for years, he still had a habit of wandering off when it suited. The night of the big event for the first lady, Denver had been seated at the head table with former president George H. Bush. During dinner, Denver had gotten up from the table and simply walked home. As Ron related all this on the drive from the airport, he was obviously still fuming that he and the Secret Service had spent hours searching for the missing honored guest.

Denver, listening in the back seat, shot back, "Mr. Ron! I lived on those streets for years! You think I can't find my way home?"

I delivered Ron and Denver to their hotel, making plans to see them later at Kim's house for the reception with sponsors. I was panicked by the thought only one of the authors would show up, but I trusted Ron to deliver Denver.

Two hours later I was unloading boxes of programs for the luncheon to the hotel ballroom where True Blessings was going to be held. I noticed Denver out in front of the hotel, with Ron nowhere in sight. My palms started to sweat.

How could Ron have left Denver alone to wander off again?

I hurried over to make sure he didn't escape. Denver was leaning against the hotel's stone facade, and he did not appear to immediately recognize me as the same woman who had picked him up hours earlier at the airport.

"White folk look alike," he would say.

Cloaked in a black shirt, black sport coat, black slacks, and signature black hat, he looked ominous. I took it as a warning sign he was preparing to slip into Charlotte's downtown and avoid the tedious meet-and-greet schedule ahead of him. I needed to think quickly to keep Denver from disappearing.

"Denver, you need a ride somewhere?" I asked.

He studied me before answering. "You got homeless people here?"

"Sure, do you want me to take you to the Urban Ministry Center?"

Why hadn't I thought of that before?

Of course I should show Denver the Urban Ministry Center; it was the perfect plan. Inspiring scenes from his book *Same Kind of Different As Me* ran through my head. I imagined taking him to the soup kitchen where Denver would surely motivate some grateful Charlotte homeless person. Denver would be motivational. Transformational. And I would get to witness it.

Denver stepped toward my minivan. As he opened the door, I reached in to move the thick folder of notes and lists filling the passenger seat. With this herculean task of lunch for one thousand, I had put my organizational skills into overdrive, filling two pages of a yellow legal pad with to-do items to check off by category and day.

As I got behind the wheel with my lists in my hands, I felt Denver examining me. I looked from his stare to my overly exact schedule and back. My anxiety clearly outlined in those lists looked a little ridiculous to me now.

"Denver, I have every minute of today scheduled, but this ride is not on the schedule," I confessed.

Denver nodded as if he already knew that, and then he flashed a grin I had not seen since he arrived.

"We are going for a ride!" he exclaimed, emphasizing *ride* in a long, southern drawl.

We arrived a few minutes later at the Urban Ministry Center in the middle of the afternoon. As we walked toward the buildings, I explained all we were doing for Charlotte's homeless. I was sure Denver would be impressed.

He wasn't.

Leading Denver on a tour of the center, I proudly gave a monologue about all of the UMC's innovative programming. In the art room dozens of paintings by homeless artists were on display. The works were vibrant in color, rich in texture, and layered with meaning.

Denver passed them without comment.

The Neighbors weren't flocking to Denver either. I had been certain Neighbors would somehow recognize this formerly homeless man, now celebrity author, and swarm us when we arrived. But everyone ignored us, intent on their own mission—surviving the day. In his dapper sport coat and hat, no one seemed to consider Denver had anything in common with them, least of all a shared history of homelessness. For his part, Denver wasn't even trying to connect his story with the homeless waiting in line.

Where was the wise man from the bestselling book?

The visit became increasingly uncomfortable. As my tour dragged on, we passed photos of our soccer team hanging on the walls. All our players competed locally and internationally while still enduring homelessness. Visitors always would remark about the players' commitment to the team in the face of this obstacle. Again, Denver had no visible display of emotion as he studied the players' proud smiles in those photos.

Moving outside the building, we came to our vegetable garden. It was at the end of the season, but Neighbors were tending collards and kale alongside volunteers. Witnessing this side-by-side interaction usually sparked conversation, but Denver peered only briefly over the fence before walking back into our main building.

Trailing behind him, I couldn't understand why Denver didn't think what we were doing was as extraordinary as most visitors did. It was maddening to think I had imagined a much different scene, sure that Denver would change someone's life at the UMC. My fantasy had been to see him wrap his arm around one of our Neighbors and whisper something utterly profound. In all honesty, I was also hoping to receive some message as well. Some praise for my ten years of dedicated volunteer service here.

Denver's silence was disturbing. Was there a message in that? Was he communicating by not speaking? I remembered one of Ron's favorite Denverisms:

> If you really serious 'bout helpin' somebody, crawl down in the ditch with 'em, bandage up their wounds, and stick with 'em until they is strong enough to crawl up on your back and get out.

Weren't we helping? All of our art, soccer, and gardening programs as well as our services were designed to build relationships with Neighbors and restore their dignity. Most cities just had soup kitchens and limited services, but in our thirteen years the UMC had developed extensive programming far beyond this basic first-aid response.

Yet Denver had not asked a single question, made one comment, or expressed a word of admiration about our innovations.

Frustrated, I turned to leave.

That's when Denver finally spoke.

Motioning to the stairway in front of us, he asked, "Can we go upstairs now?"

I was beyond frustrated. Angry even. I couldn't believe Denver was finally showing interest when there was nothing to see. "There's nothing up there. Just offices."

Denver looked from the stairs to me and then back again. All these years later I still hear his question, and the ones that followed it, as clearly as I did that day.

"Where are the beds?"

"The beds?" I asked, utterly confused.

As I started the long, complicated explanation of how Charlotte has several shelters, Denver's dark face silenced me.

Clearly, I wasn't getting his point.

"You mean to tell me you do all this good in the day and then lock them out to the bad at night?"

His accusation left me gutted.

Denver patiently allowed me my discomfort. He watched me silently wrestle with my new awareness before he quietly asked his next question.

"Does that make any sense to you?"

Of course it made no sense. I was flooded with shame.

Denver's next question would change the trajectory of my path forever. It was the question I had been waiting for and looking to answer ever since my dad died nine years before.

"Are you going to do something about it?"

I wanted to look behind me to see exactly who he was talking to, but there was little doubt. Denver was staring at me and only me. I had come here for Denver to talk to someone else. To be prophetic to someone else. To transform someone else. I was going to witness that miracle.

Now Denver was talking to me—just me.

"Do I need to say anything else?" Denver whispered.

My no was barely audible, but we both heard it loud and clear.

Steering the car back to the hotel, I tried not to look at Denver, but his words were still ringing in my ears. I had totally forgotten why we went to the UMC—to keep Denver from wandering off before the cocktail party.

Instead, he had wandered into my life and hijacked my conscience.

From the passenger seat Denver was studying me.

"You know, you don't have to be scared."

He kept talking, adding cryptically, "They already know they are coming."

"Who?" I asked, still reeling from the magnitude of his assignment.

At that moment we arrived at the hotel's circular drive.

Denver stared at me with utter certainty as he said, "The people who are going to help you—they already know they are coming."

And with that, Denver opened my car door and walked away.

———

Denver showed up for the reception that night and acted as though nothing had happened. I did too. Maybe we could just forget the whole thing.

The next morning I arrived in the hotel ballroom early with all of my lists to set up for True Blessings. My daughters were out of school for the day so they could help, and my sister Louise had flown in that morning from Washington, DC. There were dozens of volunteers assembling centerpieces and putting out programs when Dale entered the vast ballroom. Full of excitement for the day, he headed straight for me.

"Dale, I took Denver on a tour of the UMC yesterday . . ." I began.

"What did he think?" Dale looked eager to receive the same affirmation I had wanted.

"Well, that's the thing. He really wasn't impressed. He thought we should be doing more." I hesitated as Dale's face fell. "He told me we should build some beds and talked about locking them out to the bad at night."

As I floundered to find the right words, Dale tried to track my point. "Beds?" He was trying to connect the dots. "Do you mean housing? That's not what we do, Kathy."

"But maybe we should? If you had heard him yesterday, Denver was so . . ."

We were interrupted by a volunteer, and I didn't try to circle back. Dale and I would need to talk later because hundreds of guests were beginning to fill the room. My biggest concern now was whether Denver, who was supposed to inspire the crowd to give to the UMC, would tell a thousand people we actually were not doing a very good job.

Ron Hall spoke first and entertained the crowd with stories of his unlikely friendship with Denver. He was a masterful storyteller who spoke as if the thousand guests were simply friends on his living-room couch.

As Ron finished, Denver mounted the stage with all the fervor of a Southern Baptist preacher. Once more he was dressed in his signature black outfit, including his hat. Denver began softly and built to a crescendo that was part prayer and part song. The crowd had gone reverently silent as we all were now in Denver's church, and he was delivering a sermon.

Denver was his best self, stepping off the pages and bringing to life quotes from their book and gospel songs. His preaching peaked when he bellowed, "Charlotte, y'all need to do more! Y'all need to build some beds!"

I'm glad I couldn't see Dale's face in that moment. Some in the crowd seemed a little confused. Beds? Had Denver just said we should build beds? The many UMC volunteers in the room knew we didn't have a single bed. Those who were hearing about the UMC for the first time, however, seemed to take it in stride, not understanding this would be an incredible mission shift.

A longtime donor, Dave Campbell, seated next to Dale, leaned over and asked, perplexed, "Are you launching a capital campaign?"

Dale whispered back truthfully, "I have no idea what he is talking about."

Denver continued preaching, even though our event timekeeper was frantically signaling that his time was up. Denver dismissed her saying, "I see you, but I's got more to say!"

It didn't seem to matter that Denver ran on a little long because as the one thousand guests exited, they were buzzing about what felt more like a tent revival than a fundraising lunch. It didn't take long to realize everyone gave with such generosity that the Spirit must have moved the audience as well.

A small group of us led by Angela gathered in the next room we had set up as "the bank" to open piles of pledge envelopes. We gasped as we pulled out checks for $500, $1000, and even one pledge card promising $50,000.

Angela showed me another check she was holding, and we both teared up. It was one of the largest we received, and it was signed by Charlie.

I was stunned. In all the planning I'd forgotten to discuss with him what our personal pledge would be. Charlie and I had never given a gift like that to any charity. It was beyond generous. Considering our four girls and mounting tuitions, it was a little crazy.

After I picked up the phone to call him, I could hear him smiling on the other end. Although he hated receiving surprises, Charlie excelled at giving them. "I was proud of you," he said simply.

Everyone involved with planning True Blessings was realizing our gamble had paid off. Our free lunch raised over $350,000 in one hour.

It was astounding. In the thirteen-year history of the organization, the UMC had never held a fundraising event and never received pledges of that magnitude. Nonprofits all over Charlotte held fundraisers regularly for the arts or for children's causes but not to help homeless people. What exactly had Ron or Denver said to inspire so many? In all my nervousness I couldn't remember a word that had been said.

But like everyone there, I had felt the effects.

I had expected to feel a sense of relief and enormous accomplishment at the end of True Blessings. But exactly the opposite was true. At 9:00 p.m. that night, I was restless.

More restless than I had ever been in my entire life.

I had not mentioned my conversation with Denver to anyone except Dale, mostly because it felt crazy. Why was I continuing to hear the words of a formerly homeless man from Texas tell me that I should become personally responsible for housing the homeless in Charlotte?

It sounded as unlikely as building an ark, and I definitely wasn't Noah.

It was time to confess. Charlie, Louise, and I were in our den recounting True Blessing's highlights. If one of them could understand the prophetic conversation with Denver, I thought it would be Louise—the family minister. At age thirty-two, Louise had shocked us all with the revelation that she was going into the ministry and was accepted to Harvard Divinity School.

I imagined Charlie's reaction would be one of rational cynicism. What would Charlie say if he knew I thought the entire purpose of this True Blessings event was for me to meet Denver? Because of my family history of mental illness, it felt mildly dangerous to believe I should listen to Denver's voice, which I was still hearing.

I felt the conversation would go better if Louise was in the room to back me up. She had felt a calling once, so she might be able to verify this call from Denver—or dispel it.

Hesitantly I began telling them the story of how I had taken Denver on a tour that didn't go as planned. I finished with Denver's insistence that I build beds.

They both were silent.

Louise spoke first. "So you feel Denver had a message for you?"

To hear her say it sounded crazy. Maybe I just needed some sleep.

Charlie and I were brushing our teeth, standing side by side at the double sinks, looking at each other's reflection in the mirror. Silently we finished and held each other's gaze in the mirror until he spoke first.

"You know the funny thing? I'm not sure Louise got it." He paused. "But I did."

I wanted to cry with relief.

If Charlie had called me foolish or made one of his excellent rational arguments, I am sure I would have dropped the whole idea that night. At that moment, the dream of doing something was too fragile. I honestly wanted someone I trusted to talk me out of it. All it would have taken was a little loud logic to silence that brief whisper of purpose.

Instead, Charlie remembered our evening at the Outward Bound fundraiser and asked the perfect question: "So is this going to be your forty-year thing?"

I couldn't sleep that night. Denver's words more than made sense. They began to create a road map for a forty-four-year-old life that had lost direction.

The next morning I picked up Ron and Denver to take them to

the airport. I was distracted during the drive, trying to figure out a way to talk to Denver one more time before he left. I wasn't sure Denver even realized how he had disrupted my life with his charge to build beds. As they got out of my minivan with their suitcases at the airport, I pulled Denver aside before he walked into the terminal.

"Denver, can I ask you something?"

He stopped and gave me another one of his intense, unnerving stares. I had no idea if Denver even recognized me as the woman he had taken "for a ride."

"If I do this," I asked, searching for the right words, "if I build the beds, can I name it after you?"

Denver looked back at me with clear understanding and an obvious memory of our conversation. "I would like that," he said.

He then paused to consider before adding, "But you better hurry because I'm old."

ten

HOME TOUR

I do not at all understand the mystery of
grace—only that it meets us where we are but
does not leave us where it found us.

—Anne Lamott[1]

As I drove home from the airport, my mental wheels were spinning. I had just promised Denver not only to do something about the beds but to name the place after him. I was getting in deep, and I didn't even know what I was promising. What exactly was I agreeing to build? Bunk beds? Dormitories? Houses? I couldn't even picture what I was supposed to begin creating.

My sister Louise was not fazed by these questions, and she certainly was not bothered by the fact that in my midforties I was contemplating completely changing my life. The night before, when I was confessing my strange experience with Denver, Louise was remembering her own out-of-body experience, which had sharply changed the course of her life.

By the time she was thirty, Louise had already established her career as a teacher and modern dancer in Chicago. Then she began to question her own life. She found herself looking for answers in a Unitarian church, which was very different from our family's Presbyterian roots but at the same time immensely comforting. It was as if she had been on a long trip and finally come home. The sense of peace from the hymns and the thoughtfulness of the sermons left Louise fighting back tears, knowing this place had something to do with filling her emptiness.

One day the minister's message seemed explicitly written for her:

> You can sit in the pews or read the Bible all you want, but if you aren't doing anything with your faith, what are you really doing?

She knew the inner whisper she had been trying to ignore was telling her the one thing she needed to hear: you are going to be a minister.

It had been more than a little inconvenient to listen. She had to completely disrupt the life she had planned and launch herself on a course she never anticipated. Now Louise was not only an ordained minister but also had been involved for years in community organizing in DC and New York. Through many social justice projects, Louise had become familiar with public housing organizations. While I still wasn't sure if I had promised Denver bunk beds or buildings, Louise started telling me about national housing leaders I could contact for information.

It seemed laughable, really. I couldn't even believe we were talking about this. My expertise was typefaces, magazine ads, and brochures. Housing and homelessness were subjects I didn't even understand well enough to ask the right questions.

Louise knew where to start. "You should call Roseanne Haggerty with Common Ground in New York."

Haggerty grew up outside Hartford and was only seventeen when her father died, so she helped her mother take care of her seven younger siblings. In the 1980s, Roseanne Haggerty went to New York after graduating from Amherst College, and she volunteered at Covenant House—a homeless teens' charity—on 43rd Street in Times Square. Each time she walked there, she would pass the homeless sleeping in doorways on the same block where a multistory building, the Times Square Hotel, stood vacant. It made no sense to her that this available shelter was going unused while on the same block people were homeless. Roseanne kept thinking someone should do something about that.

One day she realized that someone might just be her.

Roseanne launched Common Ground in 1990, and her organization became a leader in a program called "permanent supportive housing," which combined the support services of counselors directly with housing units. It was at the forefront of a growing movement known as Housing First. The idea was that in order to end homelessness, organizations needed to shift the way people thought about helping.

Instead of expecting homeless people to "earn" their housing by becoming sober, Housing First philosophy advocated for moving the homeless directly off the streets into apartments and then providing them with the counseling, medication, and addiction treatment they might need to succeed. By having counselors work in these same housing complexes with formerly homeless tenants, services were accessible and success more likely.

Research showed this new approach was a game changer for ending homelessness. Men and women who had been homeless for years and were thought to be unreachable had dramatic improvements once they had consistent sleep, food, and medicine.

Roseanne was an early pioneer when she convinced city, state, and federal funders to use low-income tax credits to finance the purchase and renovation of the Times Square Hotel—that same empty building she had passed so often. With her vision, the Times Square reopened in 1993, transformed into a state-of-the-art apartment building with 652 homes for homeless and low-income residents. It had on-site counseling services to help residents turn their lives around. It also had a garden roof deck, a computer lab, a library, and an art studio. These amenities weren't luxuries; they were all part of a therapeutic and holistic approach to restoring someone's health and dignity after years on the streets.

Homeless residents moved in directly from the streets to a home, and case managers worked with the new tenants on mental health treatment, addictions, and disability payments. All tenants paid 30 percent of any income they earned as rent, cooked for themselves, and abided by a code of conduct. Residents could be evicted, but Common Ground understood the fact that these tenants literally had nowhere else to go. Second, third, and fourth chances were available to try to prevent someone from returning to the streets where they would most likely die.

Above all, Roseanne and Common Ground believed in the right of every human being to have a place to call home.

By 2007, when I was learning about Roseanne from Louise, Common Ground had already opened several more buildings, including another renovated hotel called the Prince George. Now considered a worldwide expert on permanent supportive housing, Roseanne and others were spreading the Housing First philosophy to cities across the country. They just hadn't made it to Charlotte yet.

When I finished reading every online article I could find, I was amazed. I couldn't believe a proven solution existed. To my knowledge, Charlotte didn't have any abandoned hotels, but there had to be a way to make this idea work. I started dreaming not about magical beds but Common Ground buildings. If I could just tour one of their buildings to see how it worked, it seemed possible to believe we could build one in Charlotte.

———

Three weeks later on a snowy December afternoon, I stood in front of the Prince George in Manhattan on 27th between Madison and 5th Avenues. Charlie and I had already scheduled our annual New York City trip for his company's Christmas party, so I decided to forgo holiday shopping for a Common Ground building tour. It was a stealth mission. No one at the UMC knew I was investigating these beds.

I couldn't have been more excited if I were heading to a Broadway show. What Common Ground had accomplished was better than a Christmas miracle—housing thousands of the hardest-to-help in only a decade.

I hesitated in front of the doorway and triple-checked the address. It certainly did not look like a place for formerly homeless people. There was no outside evidence to suggest this building was any different from a standard apartment complex. Stepping inside was an even bigger surprise—it looked like a cross between a bank lobby and a hotel. Dark wood paneling provided the background to soft sofas on my right with turnstiles straight ahead. It all looked too clean, too well appointed to fit my stereotyped vision of what might be homeless housing.

Beginning in the lobby, a Common Ground staff member took me through the multistory building, including individual apartments, a computer lab, an art studio, and music rooms.

"You'd be surprised how many talented people we have moving

in off the streets," my tour guide said as we passed a music practice room with sounds of a saxophone coming through the door.

On each floor we passed social workers' offices. Tenants could be seen talking comfortably with counselors, and often it wasn't obvious who was a staff member and who was a resident. In fact, throughout the entire building I didn't see anyone who looked obviously formerly homeless. Up the hall a clean-shaven man in a striped shirt, jacket, and blue jeans was leaving his apartment. He carefully locked his door behind him and nodded cordially as he passed us on the way to the elevator.

The realization hit me hard: once homeless people are housed, they're just people.

Homeless is an adjective that defines an extreme situation, not a human being's character.

Common Ground had found the way to change that circumstance and eliminate that stigmatizing adjective. The Prince George didn't merely suggest a different way of looking at this population but demanded it.

My guide had told me everyone pays rent, but I wasn't sure how that was possible. "You say everyone who lives here now pays 30 percent of their income for rent, but if they're mentally ill or disabled, how do they have income?"

"That has been a problem," she said with a nod. "Because of their physical and mental impairments, each tenant is eligible for disability income from the federal government, but most have never been able to complete the paperwork without the help of a case manager. That's why Housing First works. To get off the streets, chronically homeless people need a lot of help, but that can best be done when they're not starving and sleep-deprived on the streets."

When I returned to Charlotte, I could not stop thinking about what I had seen.

Homelessness seemed like a big, impossible problem, and I wasn't even sure how many homeless people there were in Charlotte. Apparently it was no one's job in Charlotte to build beds like Common Ground. And if it was no one's job, was I really willing to make it mine?

As crazy as it felt, it was already feeling crazier not to try.

eleven

MILLION-DOLLAR LARRY

The miracles in fact are a retelling in small letters of
the very same story which is written across the whole
world in letters too large for some of us to see.

—C. S. Lewis[1]

If I was really going to close my graphic-design business to work on
housing the homeless, I was going to need to convince Dale of two
things: add housing to the UMC mission statement and hire me to do it.

As a board member and volunteer, I had worked with Dale
enough to know he listened to new ideas. Months before, he had
listened to my fledgling True Blessings plan. I hoped that success
would give me credibility for this second pitch about my growing
obsession to bring the Common Ground model to Charlotte.

Unlike when I approached him for True Blessings with no real
plan, this time I would be armed with facts from my visit to New
York. I was ready to convince Dale that the UMC must begin housing.

I was unaware he no longer needed convincing.

While I was learning about Housing First in the Prince George lobby, another man named Moore, unrelated to Denver, was powerfully influencing Dale in a Charlotte living room because of a newspaper article.

A few months before Ron and Denver came to town, the *Charlotte Observer* ran an editorial written by the UMC's assistant director, Liz Clasen-Kelly. While Dale's strength in leading the Urban Ministry Center came from his ministerial background, Liz's skill was with data and public policy.

Liz had been studying Housing First for over a year before I ever heard of it, and she had tried at least once to convince Dale to implement it at the UMC. His concerns were overwhelmingly financial. Pursuing housing would cost a lot more than running a soup kitchen, and the UMC was struggling some months just to make the bread budget.

Liz did not give up. She had read a persuasive article in 2006 by Malcolm Gladwell called "Million-Dollar Murray." Gladwell wrote that homelessness was easier to solve than just manage. As evidence he offered the true story of Murray Barr, a homeless veteran living in Reno, Nevada. Gladwell argued:

> If you toted up all his hospital bills for the ten years that he had been on the streets—as well as substance-abuse-treatment costs, doctors' fees, and other expenses—Murray Barr probably ran up a medical bill as large as anyone in the state of Nevada. It cost us one million dollars not to do something about Murray.

That was what shocked Liz the most. Even after a million dollars spent on services like hospitals, drug treatment, even jail, Murray was still homeless. The system was not working for anyone, least of all the chronically homeless. The surprising fact Liz realized was this: it is less expensive to house chronically homeless people than let them die on the streets. That is how Liz decided to write her own op-ed piece for the *Observer*.

In her essay Liz used the cost of a Charlotte jail cell ($110 per night), an ER visit ($1,029 average), and a hospital bed ($2,165 per night) to show a certain Charlotte homeless man incurred costs similar to Gladwell's Million-Dollar Murray. In Charlotte, like other cities, the chronically homeless represented only 10–20 percent of the homeless population but consumed more than 50 percent of the resources dedicated to the homeless. Housing people like Million-Dollar Murray would free up the shelters to serve the 80 percent of the population that could transition out of homelessness with less intensive support.

The Charlotte man whose life and costs Liz traced to make her argument for our city was Chilly Willy, whom I now knew as William Larry Major. Liz knew if the UMC could help Chilly Willy, we would change the conversation about homelessness in Charlotte.

Liz's article and argument were powerful and prompted Dale to think about the UMC's mission. What if he could do more? What if they tried housing some people?

Dale and Liz explored some preliminary costs, but they were daunting. After the article ran, Dale got a call from John and Pat Moore, local activists and philanthropists, asking for a meeting in their home. Although John and Pat shared the same last name as Denver, there was no connection between the families.

"Liz's article made a lot of sense to me," John told Dale. "Someone should do something about it."

"I absolutely agree," Dale said feeling a little uncomfortable and wondering where this conversation was going.

"So why aren't you?" John asked.

Dale probably looked over his shoulder as I had done when Denver spoke to me.

"Me?" Dale said.

"Well, yes, you and the Urban Ministry Center. Isn't that what you do? Help the homeless?" John said. "Seems like this housing idea is the best help you could give them."

"Well, that's true, but it would be an expensive undertaking. And besides, we're a soup kitchen, not a shelter," Dale countered. "We weren't really planning on getting into housing."

"But if you were going to do something, what would you do?" John asked, not giving up.

"Um, I'm not sure," Dale hedged. "I guess we'd start a pilot program?"

"How much would that cost?" John probed.

Dale took a wild guess. "Two hundred thousand dollars."

John looked at his wife, Pat, and she nodded. "All right," John said. "We'll fund it!"

Dale was speechless. No one donor had ever given that much money to the Urban Ministry Center, much less for a program that didn't even exist. With a promise of full funding, Dale had no excuse not to try Housing First.

———

Dale and I sat across from each other in his office shaking our heads at the improbability of it all. We had each made a promise to a man named Moore to do something about housing the homeless.

"It's a God thing," Dale said.

He had certainly learned to accept this sort of divine occurrence, but I wasn't convinced. I was merely willing to admit this remarkable coincidence was about to lead to a career change.

"So we have two job openings right now," Dale informed me. "The first one is in the development office, maintaining relationships with donors and coordinating event planning. We have a lot of follow-up after True Blessings, and I think we should make this an annual event."

I nodded. True Blessings was certainly worth repeating, but I wasn't interested in taking up event planning as my profession. Maybe Dale wasn't willing to take a chance on me for something as important as the housing project. "And the other one?"

"Well, I need Liz to help run the Urban Ministry Center, so that means I need someone to start this pilot housing program," he finished with a deadpan expression.

"I want that job," I said. We both smiled.

The thought terrified me, but in my bones there was nothing I wanted more. I needed Dale to understand that I brought passion to this project but no actual experience.

"You know I am definitely not qualified for this position, right?"

Dale didn't hesitate. "The good news for you is, neither is anyone else."

I spent the rest of the holidays winding down my graphic-design business. As I called my clients to explain my job change, I was giddy. It was thrilling to finally feel unstuck. I felt that my life was in motion again, and I was ecstatic to start doing something that truly mattered.

My mom had given me a Thought for the Day calendar in my Christmas stocking. Thumbing through it, I laughed out loud when I saw this one on Day 218:

Start some big, foolish project like Noah.
—*Rumi*

—

On January 11, 2008, I drove to the Urban Ministry Center for the first time not as a volunteer but as paid part-time staff. My official contract was for twenty hours a week, but Dale and I both understood I would be working much more than that.

Liz greeted me on my first official morning with her ash-blond hair pulled back in a low ponytail. She wore blue jeans and a dazzling smile. Everything about Liz was welcoming. While I served soup to Neighbors and tried not to get involved in people's lives, Liz was the opposite, opening her office door and heart to whomever entered. Although hundreds of men and women came to the UMC each day, like Dale, Liz knew almost everyone by name. More important, she quickly earned their trust and learned their personal stories of how they had become homeless. Her small office on the first floor was constantly filled with Neighbors, the bags they carried, and their stories.

"I am so excited you are starting," she gushed. "Can you imagine if we could get Ruth a home?"

Standing barely five feet tall, Ruth's tiny figure had a large presence at the center. She worked in the UMC job program keeping order as dozens showered each day. Ruth usually reported for work in an oversized T-shirt and baggy jeans after spending the night under the Sixth Street highway overpass bridge. With little sleep and in chronic pain from severe neuropathy in both legs, Ruth was surly to Neighbors who lined up at the counter waiting patiently for their turn to take a shower. When she wasn't snapping orders, Ruth was slumped over the counter sleeping. Personally, I was terrified of Ruth. She had a way of narrowing her eyes when she looked my way that made me feel incredibly overprivileged.

"Or what about Jay?" Liz asked. "If we could promise him a place off the streets, I bet he might consider a twenty-eight-day program."

That thought made me sweat. Ruth and Jay under my watch? Jay was the loud drunk who was always ranting in the parking lot. I could not imagine trying to deal with him every day. Whenever I saw him at the front door, I went to the back entrance of the UMC to avoid confrontation.

"What about Samuel?" I asked. I needed to get some of the gentle guys under consideration. Samuel was the sweetheart with a smile.

"He would be great," Liz agreed. "Do you know Samuel has been living in the shelter for over seven years? He has nowhere to go and now he is so sick that at his last doctor's appointment they said if he kept losing weight he wouldn't make it through the year. He needs some kind of special nutritional supplement but has no way to get it."

This was the kind of information that just undid me. But Liz seemed to understand how to listen to people's burdens and not be buried by them. The hundreds of Neighbors at the UMC were all her extended family, and each brother and sister deserved a home.

"We have to consider Raymond," she went on. "He is just the sweetest man. There are over three hundred men in the shelter at night, and he just can't sleep, so he has been staying in a barn since last year. I hate that that man lives like livestock."

This was going to be a lot harder than I thought.

"I have a meeting this afternoon if you want to come," she told me. "This guy from the bank called me. He read my article and said he wanted to do something about homelessness."

Neither of us was sure what that meant, but we went late that afternoon to meet Bill Holt.

Bill's office was in one of three Wachovia bank buildings in downtown Charlotte. For years Wachovia and Bank of America were euphemistically called "Charlotte's rich uncles." If you needed something done in Charlotte, you asked for the help of one of the "uncles."

Bill had taken off his banker's suit coat and rolled up his sleeves by the time we arrived. We shook hands, and he dived into the subject of homelessness while he still stood, bouncing on his feet with excitement.

"I've been reading Liz's article," Bill began. "I think I have an idea."

On a large whiteboard he drew a rectangular outline of a building filled with circles indicating people. "I think we should build apartments for these homeless people and then, here's the thing." He added a square within his rectangle and tapped excitedly on the inner square. "We put social workers and other people who can help the homeless in the building with them."

He finished with an excited flourish and an expectant look on his face. "What do you think?"

Liz and I looked at each other, stunned.

"Bill, what you are drawing is called permanent supportive housing, and I started today to do just that," I told him.

He broke out into a huge boyish grin. "Well, I think we can get both of the banks to kick in $3 million each."

As we left, we promised Bill a place on our team—whatever that meant. In the elevator on the way down, Liz and I looked at each other and laughed. "What was that?" she asked.

As the elevator doors opened, Denver's words came back to me.

The people who are going to help you, they already know they are coming.

twelve

WING AND A PRAYER

You do not need to know precisely what is happening, or
exactly where it is all going. What you need is to recognize the
possibilities and challenges offered by the present moment,
and to embrace them with courage, faith, and hope.

—Thomas Merton[1]

The next day I went to work with the memory of Bill and his
multimillion-dollar plan on my mind. His vision of an apartment
complex was at least two years away. I couldn't begin to think about
raising money for a building yet; we still had to figure out how
to test this idea in Charlotte. At the entrance to my new office, a
vinyl plaque on my door announced our new program title with
my name:

Homeless to Homes
Kathy Izard

It was official—I really had signed up to do this. I had a desk, a chair, a computer, a window, and no idea where to start.

I spent that first month of work researching and trying to understand the landscape of homelessness in Charlotte. To my surprise, there were almost thirty agencies in the city involved in some aspect of helping those in crisis. But just like the issue of education, homelessness is a large topic with complex problems and solutions.

I began to understand distinctions between types of homelessness. Situational Homeless referred to a person or family in temporary financial crisis from a lost job or a sudden hospitalization. These families were the easiest to assist because they just needed a little help with rent to get back on their feet and into an apartment. If this happened more than once to a family, they were considered to be among the Episodic Homeless. Typically one or both of the wage earners had an issue such as mental health or addiction, and assigning a caseworker might keep the family out of constant crisis, preventing future homelessness.

Charlotte was estimated to have more than six thousand homeless persons. Our program would target the chronic homeless, thought to be only 10 percent of the total number. These were street homeless with layers of issues, mental and physical, resulting in addiction and disability. There were no families in this group. Usually the chronically homeless referred to individual men and women who had been estranged from their families and had nowhere to go. They were by definition the hardest to help and the most likely to die on the streets. I was shocked to learn that in 2007 thirty-seven homeless people had died in Charlotte. That was a number equal to the murder rate of some cities. How did this happen? It was difficult to understand how someone could stay on the streets for years.

In that first month I took a class on understanding poverty to try to comprehend how a person who has become homeless thinks and feels.

"Okay, imagine a time when there was an ice storm or power outage," the instructor said. "You have no power, no hot water in your house, and no way to cook any food. The refrigerator doesn't work, and you can't use your computer or charge your phone."

That wasn't too hard to imagine. When Lauren was nine months old, Hurricane Hugo hit Charlotte, and we had no power for ten days. It was miserable. I had to take her to the YMCA for baths, and every meal was an ordeal.

"Now imagine this has gone on for a week or more," the instructor said. "You can't sleep at night because it is so cold in your house, and you spend all day trying to figure out where your next meal is coming from and how to do something as simple as make a phone call."

The class nodded in agreement, many recalling their own Hugo stories.

"It's rough, right? All the things you take for granted—like eating, sleeping, and just staying in touch—become the focus of your day. You spend all your energy on just getting those things done, plus you're exhausted from not sleeping, right?"

He paused as we all nodded, remembering similar experiences. "So what would happen if during that time someone tried to talk with you about your IRA account?"

"I would hang up on them if I had a phone!" a man said.

The class laughed. "Right!" the instructor said. "How could you possibly listen to something about your long-term future when your immediate situation is an absolute crisis? You wouldn't care what happens in the future, only this moment, right? You can only care about the next twenty-four hours."

We all agreed.

"That is what homelessness is like," he said. "Except for many people it lasts years, not days or weeks. And no one on the streets wants to talk about getting the high-school diploma that will get them a job someday. What they need is something right now. Not next year."

This understanding was a revelation for me.

A homeless person will never tell you that what they need is a treatment program, a class, or a life strategy. Only one thing will solve their immediate, overwhelming, all-consuming crisis: a home. Our Homeless to Homes program would be Charlotte's first effort to offer the chronically homeless just that.

Dale and I met to strategize. Based on best practices in other cities we knew one social worker could effectively work with fifteen people. From the hundreds of Neighbors, we would choose fifteen men and women, move them into existing apartments, and hire one full-time case manager to work with tenants.

Dale and I believed if we did this test pilot program for two years, we would have enough data to convince potential donors of its effectiveness. That meant I had two years before I needed to worry about Bill, his $6 million plan, and building all those beds I promised Denver.

"First, we need to hire that case manager," Dale said. "And then I'm sure we can find some empty apartments to rent."

Both turned out to be much harder than we expected.

Out of dozens of candidates who applied for the social-worker position, Joann Markley was the only one who seemed to understand that this job would be 24/7—with no road map.

When I asked one applicant what he would do in a middle-of-the-night emergency with one of the pilot program residents, he looked confused. "Call 911?"

By contrast, in her interview Joann answered the same question without hesitation: "I'd get out of bed and go help them."

We hired her on the spot. Joann had worked for the county social services for years and was intrigued to help develop this new program. From the interview process, it was clear Joann was fearless. As we began the next task of finding apartments for our potential tenants, I needed her courage.

As in any city, there were neighborhoods in Charlotte we could afford and those we couldn't. Inevitably the neighborhoods where we could potentially afford rent had obvious signs of gangs or drug deals occurring on the corners. Neither bothered Joann. Where I saw danger, Joann saw opportunity.

As we roamed neighborhoods for vacancies, she would boldly march up to rental offices as I waited in my car and locked the doors. I was beginning to see that driving to the Urban Ministry Center campus was as far out of my comfort zone as I had ever gone. Not only had I hid behind the counter when I was there, I hid in my own neighborhood once I left. Charlotte had more than seventy-four zip codes, but until that month with Joann, I had probably been in only ten of them. Beyond my insular world was a larger city I had lived in for almost twenty years but knew nothing about.

"Don't you get scared?" I asked Joann.

"At first. But you learn not to be. Sure there are bad people, but there are a lot more good people than bad," she said. "Mostly you realize being poor isn't the same as being violent or criminal. It's just TV that makes us think that."

In those first few months of learning on the job, my best teacher was Joann. As we toured neighborhoods, we discussed the program, how she would work with tenants, and what we hoped would be the outcomes.

Together we drove through neighborhoods I never knew existed, looking for vacancies that met our unique requirements of low rent, low utilities, and a kindhearted landlord willing to take a chance on formerly homeless people. We were slowly realizing that combination was impossible to find in Charlotte.

I came home from one of these frustrating rental searches to a voice mail from Lynn Pearce Tate, who used to live across the street from us. Her message said she had heard what I was doing with Homeless to Homes and wanted to get together for a prayer session.

I listened to her voice mail and deleted it.

A prayer session? Not likely. I had always felt uncomfortable when people said they were praying for me.

In my adult life religion was something I actively chose to avoid. Those forced Sunday mornings and unanswered prayers of my childhood were not something I wanted to revisit. It was nice of Lynn to want to help, but prayers were not what I needed. I needed apartments.

But like Denver's words, I kept hearing Lynn's voice mail in my head. Worse, I felt guilty for not returning the call. To clear my conscience, I finally called her back, agreeing to meet. I arrived at her home early one morning after taking my daughters to school, having told no one about this meeting.

Lynn is chatty, perky, and has chin-length dark brown hair. She led me into her living room as if we were about to start book club.

"So how is Homeless to Homes going?" she asked.

I started to say, "Fine," but the honest answer slipped out. "Overwhelming."

It felt good to admit the truth. I had only been at the job a few months, but I was beginning to fully realize the magnitude of this assignment. It was hard, much harder than I had planned on, and we had not yet helped a single person.

Lynn nodded as if maybe she already knew this.

"I have found I have a gift of prayer," she said with no hesitation or awkwardness. "I kept thinking about what you were trying to do and just thought I could help."

Her words "gift of prayer" made me shift uncomfortably on the sofa. Lynn seemed confident about this gift, and I couldn't understand how or why she felt she had a direct line to God.

"So we'll just start by holding hands," she said calmly and reached over to hold my hands in hers. Lynn closed her eyes and began praying out loud.

Our hands were loosely connected, but I couldn't close my eyes. I was trying to get comfortable with this whole thing. Lynn and I had known each other for years but not like this. Our prayer meeting definitely opened a different dimension in our friendship. For a minute or two I wasn't really listening, just studying the calmness in her face as she spoke aloud. Giving in to the moment, I finally closed my eyes and tried to be as serene as Lynn.

By the time I was really hearing her words, she was finishing. "God, help Kathy find strength and wisdom for her work. Amen."

That was it. Just minutes, and it was over.

The funny thing was, it seemed my anxiety was over as well. I felt enormously relieved. I had worried this prayer get-together would feel cultish, but truly it just felt calming—like the end of a great yoga class. There was nothing scary about it, and I needed all the help I could get on Homeless to Homes.

Several times that spring Lynn and I got together, yet I never told a soul. Not even Charlie. I was afraid he'd laugh at me for believing that a prayer was going to help me do this impossible job.

Really, I didn't understand what was happening to me or why I kept returning to Lynn's condo when clearly I didn't believe in the God of her prayers. But I loved the feeling they gave me. Her home was like my private confessional booth, where I could truthfully admit things weren't going well. I could say this career change was not what I had bargained for, and Lynn would nod in understanding and she would confidently pray for me.

The experience helped me to lessen my grip on pathological

self-reliance just a little and begin to believe maybe, just maybe, I wasn't in this alone.

———

In April Joann and I finally found some apartments. They were perfect: a small cluster of one-story one-bedrooms in a quiet neighborhood with huge oak trees out front. We would be able to house up to twelve tenants in the same complex. I was thrilled, already envisioning the tenants gathering on the lawn or having barbecues outside their new homes. It had been three months since I started work, and finally we were going to be able to bring the first Neighbors off the streets.

We were finally going to do something.

Right before we signed the lease, however, our lawyer came back with terrible news: the apartments were in foreclosure. The guy I had been dealing with was running a scam, trying to steal a huge rent check before the bank took his property.

I was crushed—months of work and we were back at the starting line. It was all feeling like a giant dead end. Worse, it felt like a huge failure. I would never get this pilot program going, which meant I had no shot at building something like the Prince George.

That week I went to my prayer session with Lynn, demoralized and unsure of my next move. She listened, then held my hands.

This prayer I remember.

"God, please help Kathy know that every time you close a door, you open a window."

Later that week I met with a friend I used to work with at my first ad agency job. It had been least a year since we last talked, and I was surprised when she called. After catching up on ad agency gossip, I mentioned the difficulties in getting the program off the ground.

Unexpectedly she offered: "There is a guy at my church who has a foundation, and I think he may have a heart for this type of program. You should call him."

She thought he might help with buying furnishings if we ever found apartments. I wrote his name on a scrap piece of paper: Mark Bass. Because I was much more focused on apartments than furniture, it took me a couple of days to contact him. On Monday, April 28, 2008, Mark answered my call.

Not very practiced in asking for things, I rambled through an unprepared explanation of how I got his number and a little about the program, Homeless to Homes.

"So are you looking for apartments or money?" he asked.

Startled, I sat up in my chair. "Well, both. Why?"

"Well, I thought that was why you were calling," he said. "I have apartments."

I could not believe what I was hearing. "And you would consider renting to us?"

"Sure, let's talk."

I met Mark the next day at his apartments, but at first look, I was not optimistic. On one hand, they looked like the perfect complex I had just lost, with single-story buildings and a small grass courtyard. Most of the sixteen units, however, had huge, plywood boards covering the doors and windows. It looked like Mark thought a hurricane was coming and was overly prepared for a storm. Over the past few months, Joann and I had been to several boarded-up properties. In every case, behind the boards were rats, gang graffiti, and cockroaches.

Prying the boards loose, he apologized. "Sorry for the plywood. This is the only way I can protect the apartments from break-ins until tenants move in."

When we stepped inside, I wanted to cry.

The walls were freshly painted, the carpets were in pristine condition, the kitchens had modern appliances, and, most unbelievable compared to other apartments we had considered, they had heating and air conditioning. Not only were these ten times nicer than the foreclosed apartments I had agonized over losing, Mark was asking for less rent, and he was eager to take a chance on us. It seemed he had a deep faith, and helping people get back on their feet was something he felt called to do.

Leaving our newfound homes, I phoned Dale to tell him the good news about the ideal landlord who had just landed in our midst. Dale was thrilled but not surprised.

"God works like that," he said with a laugh.

Did he? How could Dale be so confident? I remembered my dad and his confidence in prayer leading up to Maddie's heart surgery.

God might not send you exactly what you expect, but he's always with you.

It felt like this time God had sent exactly what I needed.

Homeless to Homes finally had homes.

thirteen

TRASH AND TREASURE

It often seems, looking back, that the unexpected comes
to define us, the paths we didn't see coming and may have
wandered down by mistake. The older we get the more
willing we are to follow those, to surprise ourselves.

—Anna Quindlen[1]

It had taken almost five months to find those homes, so with all that
time to plan, I should have been more than ready. But on Saturday,
May 17, 2008, Homeless to Homes inaugural move-in day, I was a
wreck. It wasn't the truck, the boxes, or volunteers I was worried
about; it was the four people we were moving in.

Four lives now on my watch.

Choosing those lives had been more difficult than I could have
imagined. After working at the UMC every day, the Neighbors were
no longer just a sea of gray clothes and anonymous faces to me. Now,
along with Chilly Willy, I knew many of the Neighbors' names and

bits of their stories. Should we offer a home to Tyrone, who had been homeless since aging out of foster care three years ago? Or should we help Dianne, who was schizophrenic and had cycled in and out of the shelter for the past three years? To accept these two might rule out a spot for Patrick, who had epilepsy. Patrick seemed to always have a bandage on his forehead from falls on the concrete sidewalks when he suffered seizures.

After weeks of agonizing debate we did not offer Chilly Willy one of the first four apartments, though his story had been the central argument to getting this Housing First program started in Charlotte. Dale, Liz, and Joann agreed Chilly Willy was too unpredictable, and these first four tenants needed to prove that housing could work here just as it did in New York. In the end, we selected three men and one woman the UMC knew well, each at risk of dying on the streets from health issues and each highly motivated to be housed.

Just as Liz had hoped, Ruth would be the very first woman we would bring home. Along with severe neuropathy in both legs, she was living with uncontrolled diabetes and recently diagnosed gallstones. Joining her would be the other two men Liz and I had talked about on my first day of work. Raymond could finally leave that barn and Samuel would leave the shelter for the first time in over 2,500 nights. Although I had worried about accepting wild-eyed, drinking Jay into the program, he agreed to a twenty-eight-day alcohol treatment program now that he finally had somewhere to call home.

All four were grateful but skeptical about being offered a place in this new program. They each desperately wanted to come off the streets, but I am not sure any of us understood exactly what we were offering them along with their house keys. Joann would be their case manager, connecting them to services and working as their advocate on medical, mental health, and substance-abuse issues. I would keep expanding the program, finding more apartments to house more tenants. Ultimately, I would be responsible for the success or failure of this idea. In two years I needed to be able to say not only that these four were still housed, but that they were an example of what we could do for hundreds more.

The logistics for move-in day were easier to organize than this long-term goal, and my yellow legal pad was filled with notes on getting everything accomplished: four apartments—four kitchens, bedrooms, and bathrooms to stock. Our new tenants owned little beyond clothing, so this move required buying everything from toilet paper to forks to clothes hangers. I had organized a registry at Target, and friends bought bedding and bath and kitchen goods, fully stocking each new home.

I had drafted Charlie and my girls along with twenty volunteers to serve as the moving crew. The moving truck, loaded with donated furniture items, and each of the new tenants were going to meet us at the apartments. That morning, I was frantically throwing things in my car I thought we'd need. Trash bags. Paper towels. Brooms. Did we need shelf-lining paper? Would they care?

Lauren watched me, shaking her head. "It's going to be fine, Mom, really!"

I pulled out of the driveway. Charlie followed in another car loaded with more boxes along with Kailey, Emma, and Maddie. I was going over a checklist in my head when Lauren reached into the glove compartment and pulled out a CD. She put it in the player and searched for the right song. When I recognized the first few bars, I turned to look at her, my mouth open in astonishment.

She smiled at me and turned it up. "Perfect, right?"

The lyrics to "I'm Amazing," a Keb' Mo' song, started playing, and Lauren and I sang along loudly. I had used this song to make a slide show for True Blessings. As the one thousand guests had entered the ballroom, it played as background to photos of the UMC and all the amazing things that happen there. The soccer, the art, the gardening. All the things I had thought were enough. More than enough. Now, today, there would be more. Four people would no longer be homeless.

I teared up as Lauren and I belted out together with Keb' Mo' how grateful we were "for the simple things" that we don't ever stop to think about.

I was so grateful for this new path that had unstuck me from my safe world. I had no idea what was ahead, but I knew that today felt amazing.

No one could stop smiling all day, least of all me. As volunteers helped Raymond, Samuel, Ruth, and Jay move in, it was eye opening how few possessions each owned and how they carried these items to their new homes. No suitcases or boxes. Just green plastic garbage bags holding all they had in the world. Salvaged clothes and shoes, a few toiletries, maybe a wrinkled four-by-six photo. Each new tenant was over forty years old, yet from four decades of living, these few plastic bags were the only evidence of that life.

Ruth, Raymond, Samuel, and Jay moved through their new homes with disbelief. Mark's apartments were simple two-bedroom apartments with front doors opening onto a grass lawn. The new tenants kept coming in and out in astonishment.

"This is my own garden?" Raymond asked. "How about that! I am going to plant me some tomatoes!"

"Y'all come see my house," Ruth said, inviting each volunteer.

"I can't believe I will be able to watch movies and not have to fight with all the other guys in the shelter." Samuel shook his head in wonder.

At bedtime I was exhausted, but I couldn't sleep. At first, the day's happy images scrolled in my head like a Disney movie with the Keb' Mo' soundtrack playing in the background.

Raymond marveling at his own bathtub. Samuel opening and closing his refrigerator door. Ruth testing the softness of her couch.

It really had been a remarkable day.

Panic woke me at 2:00 a.m. I was used to waking up at night worried about my teenage daughters—were they home? Did they make their curfew? But this night I was wide awake worried about my new family; I now had four new "teenagers" in my life. What if Raymond, unfamiliar with his new stove, had started a fire in Mark's apartments? What if newly sober Jay was having a party in his apartment? How would I explain that to our donors, the Moores?

Monday morning I arrived at the UMC full of dread, expecting Joann to fill me in on some horrible happening, but I couldn't find her. Ruth was in her usual place monitoring the shower counter. She waved at me.

Ruth never waved at me. She was also smiling, wide awake, and neatly dressed in a clean shirt with a necklace. Necklace? I had never seen Ruth wear a fashion accessory.

Cautiously, I walked over to talk with her. "Hey, Ruth!"

She gave me a huge, unprompted, first-time-ever hug. "Kathy!"

"How were your first two nights?" I asked.

"Did you see how it rained yesterday?" she asked. I nodded, not sure why that mattered.

"It rained yesterday and I didn't get wet!" Ruth marveled.

I found out there were no parties that weekend, no incidents. Raymond confided he spent the whole weekend filling his bathtub with Mr. Bubbles, soaking until the hot water cooled, then doing it all over again. Looking at the photos from that move-in day, I framed one to keep on my desk. In it, all the move-in volunteers surround Ruth, and her smile is electric. It was a constant reminder that whenever it rains, at least now, Ruth doesn't get wet. And Raymond gets wet by choice in his own bathtub.

I made a silent vow to myself that in two years, by 2010, there would be a picture on my desk of dozens more smiling, dry Ruths and freshly showered Raymonds with places to call home.

———

The same month I helped move Ruth and her two garbage bags into her home I also moved dozens of garbage bags out of my mom's house. It had taken over a year, but we had finally sold our childhood home, and Mom was moving into a senior-living community. My sisters and I were certain we were doing the right thing because the maintenance on our four-bedroom home had become overwhelming, but Mom wasn't convinced.

In her mind we had just made her homeless.

I traveled to El Paso early for the clean-up, and my sisters planned to join me for the actual move later in the week. Organizing and sorting were my strengths. Faced with the mounds of possessions stored during forty years in our home, I was sure I could be the most efficient in sorting trash from treasure.

It was easy to see Mom wasn't happy about this move she had agreed to months ago. She had promised to begin the process of cleaning out, but as I looked around the kitchen, I could see she had done nothing.

I sighed, looking at it and wondering how we were going to move and clean it all in the allotted week. Mom admitted, "I just didn't know where to start."

My mom loved this house and everything in it. It had stayed relatively unchanged since 1969. Even the kitchen appliances were still avocado green, because over the years Mom found someone to custom paint when she need a new refrigerator or dishwasher. One of the few things that had changed in our house was my room. Both Allyson's and Louise's bedrooms were basically untouched from the time they were thirteen. Dad had turned my room into an office shortly after I was married. As a result, I stayed in one of my sisters' rooms when I came to visit Mom. It had always bothered me that my room was sacrificed for this purpose. Why not use Louise's room? She had been out of the house longer than me.

This visit, the last visit to my childhood home, it mattered even more.

As I walked around wondering where to begin, it struck me that this house had stopped feeling like my home, my haven, a very long time ago.

In what used to be my room, the bed under my window had been replaced with a huge wooden desk. Dad's tennis trophies and accomplishments had been moved from the den to this upstairs office. I wanted to sit in the chair across from Dad's and tell him about the last few months. About Denver, my new job, about my momentous moving day the week before.

I am doing something, Dad. I am finally doing something.

I hoped, somehow, he knew.

My closet door was open, and I stepped inside. My seventh-grade cheerleading uniform was hanging next to my old tutus and my high school letter jacket. I stepped up on the shelves so I could peer into the secret fort at the top of my closet. My baby pillow was still up there, and Snoopy smiled back at me.

I felt a wave of homesickness. I reached for Snoopy and brought him down with me to hug his neck. It was time I took him home—to Charlotte. Snoopy accompanied me down to the kitchen to start the serious work of cleaning out. When I opened a cabinet by the telephone, rolls of wrapping paper, ribbon, and bags of cards spilled onto the floor. Here was my mother's Hallmark addiction. My childhood friend Andrea now owned the card store in El Paso, and my mom was her best customer, shopping there at least twice a week. For each birthday, anniversary, Easter, Mother's Day, Halloween, and Valentine's Day, Mom sent a separate card to each of our girls, Charlie, and me. That was about twenty-five cards a year to my family alone. Then there were my sisters, my aunts and uncles and their children, and now their children's children. There were dozens of bags of cards from Andrea's store. Mom loved buying extras just in case. She was like a holiday Girl Scout—always ready.

This habit slightly annoyed me. Why did she spend so much time on it? She spent hours every week buying, writing, and mailing these cards. Her dedication baffled me. I knew she would want to take every card and ribbon to her new home, but I was going to be ruthless. There was no way we were boxing all this and moving it. Mom would just buy it all again anyway.

Sort. Sift. Save. Discard. Sort. Sift. Save. Discard.

I got more frustrated as I opened more drawers and cabinets. More Hallmark paraphernalia poured out. Some rolls of wrapping paper were brand new, never opened. Some were half used and bunched. The half-used rolls I stuffed in trash bags, and the brand new I set aside.

The bags piled up, and I dragged them past Mom to get to the garage.

"What's all that?" she said, alarmed.

"Oh, you know, kitchen junk," I said vaguely.

It was amazing to think each tenant in Charlotte had only two bags of treasure, yet I could fill two of those same trash bags in only one room of my mother's house.

I moved upstairs to Mom's bedroom and began cleaning out the bathroom vanity. There were only two drawers, a his and hers.

I knew my dad's things were still in his, even though he had been gone for nine years. I opened hers first expecting to quickly sort, sift, save, and discard the contents. When I opened the drawer, however, my father's handwriting stared up at me from the corner. It stopped me cold. His neat script was unmistakable. Dad had precise penmanship, always measured and slanting right in even, sure strokes.

I reached down to touch his handwriting on the top card and then picked up the stack of cards bound with a rubber band. I didn't count them, but I knew there had to be over thirty cards. They were the standard two-by-three-inch innocuous white cards a florist sends with flowers. In this case I knew a dozen red roses had accompanied each card. The same flower, the same color, and the same dozen my dad had been sending my mom every year on their anniversary, just like he had since college. Each card read: "All my love, Leighton."

Each card written by my dad. Each card saved by my mom. For over thirty years.

I sat down on the stool at my mom's vanity. Each action was remarkable: that my dad had handwritten each card. Had he driven by the florist before they delivered them? That my dad never wavered and sent the same dozen red roses each year to remind my mom of his steadfast love, even during their most difficult years. That my mom saved each card, now a two-by-three-inch record of their love story.

Charlie sent me flowers on our anniversary, my birthday, and Mother's Day, always from my favorite florist. Different arrangements each time—hydrangeas, tulips, roses—different colors and different buds according to the season. I loved that he did that. I loved the surprise of not knowing what would show up on my door, always certain he wouldn't forget. Charlie's cards were always different too. They would be typed from the florist with different messages that Charlie dictated over the phone. For our first anniversary: "That wasn't such a bad year, was it? Love, moi."

Or another favorite, harkening back to our first-date story: "You wouldn't want to have a beer with me, would you? Love, moi."

We had over twenty anniversaries now, but I had not saved one of those cards. My girls would never open a drawer and find the witness to our love story. It would be only ours to know. Charlie and I both easily threw things away. Our house was neat and tidy. No stacks of anything anywhere. Looking at the sweet stack my mom had saved, I regretted throwing away Charlie's cards to me. I regretted some of the other things I had discarded over the years. It made me sad to know I had made something trash before it had the chance to be treasure.

I thought about our girls and their future love stories. Would they be romanced by flowers and cards? Or would they only have texts as witness to their stories? They couldn't say to their kids, "Look at the first text your dad ever sent me."

I held the cards in my hand, the thirty years of love radiating from them. I may have had enormous uncertainty in my life growing up. I may have had sadness in never knowing the mom I could have had. But I had always been surrounded by a love that was truly rare. And that love had made this old house a home.

I carefully placed the cards back in the drawer. Mom would want to pack these herself.

fourteen

PRAYING TO A GOD YOU DON'T BELIEVE IN

Man is born broken. He lives by mending.
The grace of God is glue.

—Eugene O'Neill[1]

"Hey, Jay," I said as he got into my car.

Jay nodded shyly at me as he fastened his seatbelt. The wild man I used to avoid at the Urban Ministry Center was freshly shaved and wearing a knit shirt. I had never seen Jay this clean or this calm. Before moving in with Homeless to Homes, Jay's difficulty conversing with others and his struggles with alcoholism had led him to drink to oblivion. Now, after nearly two months of sleep and sobriety, Jay was a serene, grateful passenger in my car. It was difficult to remember this was the same man who would drunkenly shout in the UMC parking lot only months ago.

Joann had asked me to take Jay to buy groceries. While I was happy to help, I was uncomfortable at the same time. Jay and I didn't know each other, and this shopping trip was going to stretch the limits of our conversational capabilities. Jay probably would have been fine to ride quietly, but I felt the need to talk in order to break the awkward silence.

"How's your place?" I asked.

"Fine, ma'am," Jay said with bright eyes that made him look like a happy kid bursting with the best secret. "Real nice."

Jay's apartment was next door to Samuel's, so I thought that might be a line of conversation. "How's Samuel?"

"He's fine."

"A good neighbor?"

"Yes, ma'am, real fine."

I wasn't sure what else to ask him, so we drove in silence the rest of the way to the grocery store.

Frank's Supermarket was not like the grocery store in my neighborhood. There was no mini coffee shop as we entered, no delicatessen with fancy cheeses, no café tables. The produce section was not overflowing with exotic options, like kiwi and passion fruit. Just the basics, like apples, oranges, onions, potatoes, and tomatoes. The shelves were not bulging with products, and the aisles did not have colorful promotions encouraging the consumer to stock up for the latest holiday. This was a utilitarian grocery store, and many shelves were bare. I had never seen such an empty store in my neighborhood, except in the aftermath of Hurricane Hugo.

Jay pulled a wrinkled list from his pocket and began methodically filling it. I was a little self-conscious tagging behind him in the aisles, but it got easier as I asked him questions about his purchases.

"Are those collards?"

"Yep," he said, looking at me funny. "You didn't know that?"

"No, Jay, I'm from West Texas," I admitted. "I have never seen or eaten collards."

"What?" He laughed. "You fooling me?"

"Nope. My mom didn't cook them, and I've never made them. Never ordered them either."

"What? You are missing something!" he said and started to explain how he cooked them, just like his mama used to make them steeped with backfat and Vidalia onions.

We continued through the aisles, getting other things I had never shopped for: black-eyed peas, ham hocks. The whole meat cooler was a revelation. Beef tongue? Did they even sell that in my store? What was most eye opening was the way Jay shopped. When I went to the grocery store, I hurried through, throwing things in my cart as fast as I could, not checking prices or even caring if it was on my list. Maddie and Emma would always attempt to hide things in the cart when I wasn't looking, hoping the Cocoa Puffs and cheese balls would make it through unnoticed at the checkout line.

Jay was deliberate and thoughtful. It finally occurred to me he was painstakingly doing the math as he shopped, making sure the total would match the dollars in his pocket. At the checkout counter he added cigarettes almost as a reward for staying within budget.

We loaded his things and got back in my car.

"Jay, you seem to be doing really well since you got out of treatment."

"Yes, ma'am, I think I am," he said, making that pleased secret smile again.

We rode in silence a minute.

"You know, growing up my sister told my mama she heard voices in her head," he said. "My mama let them send my sister to the state hospital. When she came back, I didn't even recognize her. I don't know what they did to my sister in there, but I never told my mama I heard voices too. I just started drinking. That made them quieter."

I glanced over at Jay, but he was staring out the passenger window. That brief glimpse into his world said everything about poverty, mental illness, and homelessness. A drink might drown the voices until they drowned you. I knew my mom heard voices, but that was the first time I considered the fact that she had never turned to a bottle to escape. She had turned to the pages of her Bible instead. Our lives would have been much more complicated had she chosen differently.

———

Jay's newly achieved sobriety was a marked change, and each Homeless to Homes tenant that summer was going through similar transformations. Just as the Prince George tenants didn't *look* homeless, our residents were returning to "normal" in those first weeks too. Each resident, once they had a solid month of sleep, food, and showers, looked remarkably well. Clear eyes, combed hair, clean clothes, and reduced drinking softened them into four surprisingly average tenants.

They began asking Joann for help with issues they could never address while homeless. Ruth saw a dentist for the first time in her life. Raymond got his first pair of eyeglasses. Jay met with a psychiatrist and finally got a prescription to help with those voices he heard. But the metamorphosis of Samuel was one of the most dramatic.

After living in the men's shelter for seven years, Samuel had a long list of health problems. With Joann's help he received much-needed medical care and could finally take his medicines consistently for the first time in years. His diet improved as well now that he cooked for himself and took nutritional supplements.

Samuel was the first of the four tenants to express an interest in doing something more productive with his days. Now that he was no longer in survival mode wondering where his next meal would come from, Samuel had time to reflect and imagine a different life for himself. Samuel imagined he'd like to go back to school.

Joann helped him enroll at the community college in a math course that would be the first step on the path to his GED, the high-school-equivalency degree. Samuel regretted not graduating, and he was going to take care of that now. He had been in class a few weeks when I saw him at the UMC.

He was in the dining room at lunch, sitting at a table talking with some Neighbors who had obviously known him awhile. Samuel was clean shaven, wearing a white knit shirt, knee-length plaid shorts, and basketball shoes. He casually slung his backpack over his shoulder. For the first time, it wasn't full of clothes or food—just a couple of books for his math class. Samuel was clearly enjoying the positive attention and his almost celebrity status.

I smiled as I watched him. He was so proud of his new path. Lauren would be starting her freshman year at Vanderbilt University in a few weeks. Although it was late summer, she constantly wore the sweatshirt we had purchased in the bookstore when we visited her dream school last year. Now, every time she talked about heading to Nashville, her face lit up and her smile full of promise stretched across her face just like Samuel's.

A longtime UMC staff member who had known Samuel for years came up beside me.

"I cannot believe that is Samuel," she said, shaking her head. We watched him together a minute more before she spoke again. "I always thought he was a lost cause."

That was our lesson that summer. No one was a lost cause.

At the time, I never fully envisioned that housing could produce such radical change. Promising Denver those beds, I had imagined only a more comfortable living situation for the street homeless—a more humane circumstance. I didn't have the faith to consider that people really would change given the chance.

Every day those four Neighbors proved me wrong. Having a home wasn't just about comfort; it was true conversion. Just as Denver had been transformed from thirty-years homeless into a best-selling author, possibility resided in every single life we could touch.

Samuel and each of the Homeless to Homes tenants were demonstrating that housing represented hope. We didn't need to wait two years to "prove it." We had our proof.

It was like having the cure for cancer but waiting two years to give it to more people.

Dale and I decided we should move up the timetable with a two-tiered strategy. We would continue to fill the pilot program, but with only thirteen tenants, not fifteen, saving some money so we could also move ahead with developing our own building.

Scaling back from fifteen to thirteen pilot-program tenants made each choice even more critical. For the time being, only nine more people would receive the gift of hope and housing that Raymond, Samuel, Ruth, and Jay now shared.

We tried to be systematic about it, considering specific factors for each potential candidate: years on the street, health risks, background. But the truth was, so much emotion was included in all those harsh facts. There were so many layers, hundreds of stories that we couldn't know until we met with each potential candidate. Joann did most of the interviewing and tried to select the neediest cases.

After one particularly heart-wrenching interview, Joann sat down heavily in the chair across from me. "I know I don't really get a pick," she admitted, "but if I had one, this would be my guy. There's something special about him."

She was talking about Eugene Coleman, and he had been coming to the UMC since it opened in 1994. I am sure I served him dozens of times in the soup line, but because I was trying to hide behind the counter, I hadn't noticed that he thought he was invisible too.

———

"Got a cigarette?"

Eugene Coleman looked up from his sleeping bag at his camp-site, a filthy hole of a place under a highway overpass near downtown Charlotte. He had a cigarette, but he wasn't about to share it with this guy. "Sorry," he said and turned his back, trying to rest his head on his arm. It was the middle of the day, but Coleman needed to get some sleep. The nights were brutal: trains rolling by, cars overhead. The worst was trying to sleep with one eye open so that in the middle of the night nobody took what little he had. Coleman had been beaten more times than he could remember defending his campsite. It was what you did on the streets to survive, and it had been his life now for longer than he could remember.

Coleman had been one of twelve children growing up in Winnsboro, South Carolina. He was the firstborn male after five daughters, but as the number of mouths to feed grew to a dozen, his exalted status wore off. With no father and bored with school, Coleman left home at fifteen to live with his uncle Leroy, traveling the South working a series of construction jobs. Along the way he fathered a son, Elkin Eugene Smith, but he drifted out of his boy's life, moving from one construction job to another.

Eventually he worked his way up to supervisor at a carton com-pany. Coleman loved the physical labor, and when the forklift was too tedious he oftentimes used the quicker method of lifting ship-ments with his strong back. Through this manual labor, Coleman developed a hernia, which required a simple surgery. But that opera-tion was the beginning of a long, dark slide for Coleman.

When he came out of the anesthesia, he knew immediately something was wrong. Coleman couldn't feel anything below his waist, and doctors confirmed he was temporarily paralyzed. The spinal tap used to anesthetize him had gone horribly wrong. After three or four weeks in the hospital, he could finally sit up without pain and go home, but his life was forever altered.

Along with drastically limited mobility and dependence on pain medication, Coleman took home an intense distrust of doctors. He swore no one would ever operate on him again.

Back at work Coleman could not be the hardworking supervisor he once was. The pain dogged him, and he took more medicine than prescribed to numb it. Months later he developed a new problem—a cyst had started to grow on his left shoulder. At first only Coleman noticed it, but each month it doubled in size. Soon his employers questioned what was on his shoulder, and each time Coleman prom-ised to get it looked at but didn't. There was no way he was going back to a doctor and risk another surgery. It started to become pain-ful, and using his shoulder was more and more difficult.

As the cyst grew, so did Coleman's lies to himself and those around him. He missed days at work to stay home and relieve his pain by drinking and smoking pot. Escaping with substances also numbed the fear of going back to a hospital to remove the cyst, which was now the size of a baseball.

The downward spiral that began with a botched hernia proce-dure hit bottom when Coleman lost his job, his income, and then his apartment. He became homeless sometime in the early 1990s. After that, Coleman came to the Urban Ministry Center every day for food but rarely talked to anyone. He resigned himself to his home-lessness and living under a bridge, the place he called "the hole I lived in."

Coleman thought things couldn't get worse until he read a newspaper obituary in a random copy of the paper he'd picked up on the streets he wandered. The death notice was for Elkin Eugene Smith, his son, shot dead at seventeen.

The hole got blacker and deeper after that.

With no calendar, no family, and no purpose, the years bled into each other. It all changed that day the stranger asked him for a cigarette. As Coleman was turning away, trying to get comfortable in his sleeping bag, he heard the man say, "I got a train to catch."

Minutes later he heard that train start rumbling through—a noise he had heard every day, several times a day for years. But this time it was different. This time over the deafening roar of the train, he could hear screaming. Coleman ran down the tracks but soon wished he hadn't. The man who wanted a cigarette and had a train to catch had been cut in two after falling on the tracks. That blood-ied, dead body was a startling wake-up call for Coleman.

Lying awake that night, Coleman prayed to a God he didn't believe in. "Lord, I don't want to die out here like this."

He wasn't sure how to get himself out of that hole, but he knew he was going to need help. And he didn't like asking for help. He heard rumors at the soup kitchen that the UMC had started housing homeless people. Coleman had been going there for years and never heard anything like it. Sounded like a scam to him. Probably rich people trying to make money off the backs of poor people. But he took a chance. He wasn't going to die out here.

"Excuse me, ma'am, you got a minute?" he said to Joann. "Are you the lady that gets people off the streets?"

I still have a photo of Coleman taken the day he moved into his

Homeless to Homes apartment. In the picture he has short dread-locks fanning out under his baseball hat. After twenty years on the streets, his eyes were wildly bloodshot, but his grin, missing many teeth, stretched across his entire face. Joann had just handed him a key. Nothing fancy, just the standard silver key that looked like any other on a plain stainless-steel ring.

Coleman had stared at it in his palm in amazement. "I can't remember the last time I had a key to anything," he said.

He held up the key with two fingers in his right hand and smiled as I took the photo.

The camera didn't capture his words, but I will never forget them.

"This is a Kodiak moment!" Coleman said.

Coleman's story was one of the first that helped me truly understand how homelessness might happen to someone. Before I met him, on some level I believed the myths that some people chose to be homeless or that they liked living outside or that they had done something to deserve their situation. Coleman had been rising above the home he grew up in, just a working guy, when a medical mistake altered his life forever.

Certainly there were twists in his story, different choices he could have made, but it began with a blindsiding collision with the unexpected. That, I understood.

fifteen

HOME ALONE

Perhaps home is not a place but simply
an irrevocable condition.

—James Baldwin[1]

The Neighbors at the center no longer felt like strangers now that I was there every day, learning their stories. Chilly Willy regularly greeted me in the parking lot. Like Jay, Chilly Willy used alcohol to drown voices and memories. On a good day he would proudly say he was going to be a sober man, but on a drinking day Chilly Willy could keep a person tied up in his dysfunction. One day it was clear that Chilly had been attempting some serious drowning, and his buzz was wearing off.

Sitting with him on an outside bench, I didn't really know where to start with Chilly Willy, but I knew he needed to be heard. The only details I knew about Chilly's life I had learned in pieces from his brother, Johnny, and from Liz. Chilly once had a girlfriend who was killed, but I didn't know the specifics. That day Chilly Willy willingly filled in those blanks and many others with unnerving honesty.

"You know my daddy was a preacher."

I was stunned. "Really?"

"Yep." Chilly shook his head and looked away. "He didn't know what to make of me."

We let that sit between us.

"I had a wife once too. Her name was Crystal. She was two months pregnant when she was hit by a car and died. Some days, all I want is a good Christian woman and a guitar," which he pronounced *gee-tar*, with a thick southern accent and a laugh. "But look at me, what good Christian woman would marry me?"

We were quiet a moment. It was hard to imagine this gentle bear of a man pining for love could also be the same guy who had gone to prison at seventeen.

"Mom!"

My twins, Maddie and Emma, now teenagers about to enter high school, were headed toward us from the parking lot. Their summer job was volunteering for the UMC: organizing mail, filing records, and serving during lunch. Today, they were finishing up a mural they had painted in my office. The entire wall facing my desk was now a giant kaleidoscope of color leading to these words in the center: *Amazing! Keb' Mo'.*

They decided to paint that reminder on my office wall so I would never forget that first True Blessings and that first move-in day.

"Hey, pretty girls!" Chilly Willy said. "Can I have a hug?" Maddie and Emma smiled and dutifully gave Chilly Willy a one-arm hug with one twin on each side.

"This your mama?" he asked.

"She is!" Maddie told him.

"You do like she tells you," Chilly Willy told them solemnly. "I didn't listen to my mama at your age and look how I turned out."

—

Sadly, Chilly Willy was not one of the final tenants chosen for Homeless to Homes. We worried he was still too unpredictable to live in an apartment without twenty-four-hour security as the Prince George building I'd visited in New York has. Gradually we filled all the remaining spots in the pilot program. Coleman, Teddy, Johnny, Edna, Chuck, Debra, TJ, James, and Christine all moved off the streets and came home.

The program operated quietly in Mark's apartments and two other units in another part of the city. We didn't announce our presence in either neighborhood for a reason: all thirteen were no longer homeless—they were housed. They were now just people who had finally lost the stigma of that word *homeless* and were trying to quietly rebuild their lives.

They ate, they slept, and they tried to remember what it was like to feel human again.

Coleman entered the UMC substance-abuse treatment program and became its first graduate who also was a tenant with Homeless to Homes.

Raymond did an interview with a local radio station. "What's your favorite part of your new home?" the reporter asked.

"The mailbox!" he said. "I love getting mail in my own mailbox! I even love getting junk mail. It makes me feel like a human again."

I think I somehow believed it would be that easy. Move in. Start life. Get mail. Live happily ever after. It was Raymond who let me know it wasn't that simple.

He was on his front porch tending his new tomato plants when

I stopped by the apartments. Sitting on his concrete steps, he clearly looked lonely.

"You okay?" I asked.

Raymond shrugged, his silence speaking volumes, since he always had something to say. Joann was busy with another tenant, so I tried my best to help.

"You want to talk?"

Raymond hesitated, but decided I would be an acceptable substitute for Joann. "I just miss the center is all."

That surprised me, to say the least. I couldn't imagine why Raymond missed all the people, the lines, and the struggles of street life.

"I had friends there," he said simply.

"Raymond, you can go to the center anytime," I assured him.

The UMC was about a mile-and-a-half walk or an easy bus ride from his new apartment. We assumed tenants might visit for the art or gardening programs—another reason the proximity of these apartments was so perfect.

Raymond shook his head. "I can't be there anymore. I feel too guilty."

I was confused. "Why do you feel guilty?"

"My friends are still on the streets. I have a home and they don't," he explained. "I can't help them either."

Now I understood. Raymond had gained a home but lost his family.

As difficult as life is on the streets, homelessness creates camaraderie. People who have nothing share something with each other. Even if they don't share their true identity, they are well known to each other by street names: Chilly Willy, Dancing Bear, Peanut. On the streets, just as in high school or a workplace, natural groups form and friendships develop. People share things as small as cigarettes and as big as campsites.

From this "street family" we had housed only thirteen men and women. These people had dozens of friends, and in some cases blood relatives, still on the streets. Raymond and the other twelve Homeless to Homes tenants had all signed the same lease agreement, which stated no one could come live with them. It was a requirement to keep order in the apartments. If our tenants allowed others to move in who were not part of the program, each resident in our program risked losing his own housing.

We had chosen thirteen people to win this housing lottery. While they all might have known each other on the streets, they weren't necessarily friends. Each was also struggling with his or her own readjustment to a typical life. In selecting tenants, I had never considered the community that we would disrupt or the new one that needed to be built. Raymond was housed now, but other than those in our program, anyone else he might befriend could never understand where he'd been. How could Raymond explain that his residence before this had been a barn? How could he make new friends with people who had no frame of reference for what he had endured the past few years?

Raymond had made steady progress since moving in, but now that he didn't wake up every day frantic about survival, he had time to consider his life.

Right now, his life was decidedly lonely.

Just as I had not envisioned our tenants' quick progress in some areas, I had not imagined the depths of their struggles moving beyond the stigma of homelessness. Although Raymond was now safe inside, he carried a tremendous shame related to how he got there. His euphoria upon moving in had given way to isolation and depression.

I was beginning to fully appreciate that while it was remarkable progress to save thirteen people from the streets, housing and living were two completely different matters.

———

"Hey, Mom," I said in my weekly phone call. "What's new?"

"I signed up for the trip to China with the museum!" Mom said.

"Really?" I asked. The idea made me equally proud and terrified.

I was impressed that she was going to fulfill this lifelong dream. Ever since my dad died Mom had become increasingly independent. We had all worried that when he was gone Mom would have to be hospitalized again, but it hadn't happened. Even though Mom was doing well, she still struggled intermittently and I had never shaken the worry that a hospital stay was around any corner. What would we do if the long plane ride to Asia triggered a chemical imbalance while she was in Shanghai?

"There's a nice group going from El Paso, and we are even going to see the Terracotta Warriors!"

"Wow, Mom, what an adventure! That's going to be great," I said, while secretly worrying how long it would take me or my sisters to board an emergency flight to Beijing. "What are you doing today?"

"Well, I need to go to the store and get some more supplies for my bags," she said.

Ever since Mom read *Same Kind of Different As Me*, she had started her own campaign to help the homeless. She kept plastic bags in her car that had a bottle of water and small cans of food. When she saw someone at a stoplight asking for help, she would give them a bag.

"Then I'm probably going to my office."

I smiled. Her office was Andrea's card store. Mom would go in to buy her cards and then set up on one of the back tables intended for customers who were picking out wedding invitations. Mom sometimes even took her lunch with her—a smoothie or milkshake from Baskin-Robbins. She had a desk in her new apartment, but she still didn't feel at home there. Ever since we had moved Mom into senior living, she spent most days trying to leave it. Not running away, just spending every minute she could somewhere else.

Mom still drove to the same beauty shop fifteen minutes away even though there was a service in her building. Her daily routine became fixing herself breakfast and then leaving midmorning for the beauty shop, the bank, the nail salon, the grocery store, the post office, the card store, the church—anyplace for an errand. Pretty much anywhere but there suited her.

Our weekly phone calls usually began with news of her book club or bridge group before a side comment about her new living arrangement.

Mom constantly dropped subtle hints that she was the youngest, most active person in her new apartment community. "I went to visit my ninety-two-year-old friend down the hall yesterday."

She rarely told me anything about someone, except his or her age. I accused her of age profiling.

"How is your program going?" she asked.

"Well, pretty good," I said. "A few tenants are having a hard time adjusting, you know. Even though it's better than being homeless, I think getting used to life in a new apartment is really hard. Nothing feels familiar."

"I know," Mom said.

I hung up the phone, feeling humbled. It seemed my mom and Raymond were both teaching me some hard lessons about housing. It takes more than four walls and a bed to make a place feel like home.

sixteen

CHRISTMAS MIRACLES

Christmas doesn't just come in neatly wrapped presents. It
comes in our beautiful messy attempts to love each other.

—Becca Stevens[1]

Along with hard lessons I was slowly realizing this project was much
bigger than I had planned. Seven months into this Homeless to
Homes experiment, we were convinced we needed to build our own
apartment complex, but Dale and I both knew finding land, building apartments, and running a program for one hundred people was
going to take expertise neither Dale nor I had.

"This is going to take more than a graphic designer and a minister," I told Dale.

So far our *team* consisted of only Bill Holt, the $3 million–
dreaming banker. Dale and I brainstormed about friends who had
the skills we needed. Matt Wall (real estate), Jerry Licari (business), Downie Saussy (construction), Hugh McColl III (finance),

and David Furman (architecture). Throughout the next few years I would refer to them as my Five Guys.

Our first assignment was an exploratory mission to evaluate all the possible sites. It was a dream team expedition to be sure. We were shopping for land that cost hundreds of thousands of dollars with absolutely no way to pay for it, in neighborhoods that surely would not want us. With six of us in an SUV, we'd slowly drive by properties and comment on the merits of a site.

David, as the architect, carried the most weight. In my mind we would go with what he liked, until I realized he liked a two-acre junkyard full of rusting cars with a giant radio cell tower looming hundreds of feet in the air over the mounds of scrap metal.

"Are you kidding?" I asked him. "With that radio tower?"

"I like it!" he said. "It's like yard art!"

"Well, it's the least expensive," Dale agreed. "And it's right near our Homeless to Homes apartments, so we know the neighborhood."

Matt was charged to investigate further and get ready to make an offer.

Returning to my office, I saw the quote I had taped to my computer from last Christmas's word-of-the-day calendar:

Start some big, foolish project like Noah.

It seemed we were doing just that. Our team put together a preliminary budget with land, construction, and some start-up operating costs: $10 million. Ten million.

I wasn't sure which was more improbable—the junkyard or the budget.

———

In the fall of 2008, the recession was starting to sink the national psyche. Even if we could dream of raising $10 million someday, we needed $500,000 right now so we could buy land and have a site ready to build on.

Dale and I brainstormed in his office.

"What about the City of Charlotte?" I asked. "Shouldn't there be a line item in the city budget for this?"

Dale shook his head again. "We've never gotten any traction with the city. And to ask for city money, we have to own the land first."

"And to own the land we need the money!" I finished his thought. "To raise money from donors we need a site, and to buy a site we need money, but to get money we need—"

"A miracle," Dale said. We sat for a while in frustration before Dale offered, "You know, maybe I could call Dave Campbell."

Dave headed a family foundation and had been present at True Blessings when Denver shouted that Charlotte needed to build some beds. Dale set up a meeting with Dave, and when we arrived, I was so nervous I could barely speak. I had never asked anyone for money, much less a six-figure gift. We came prepared with a sketch David Furman had created of our three-story apartment dream on the two-acre junkyard property.

Dale led our meeting with compelling stories from Homeless to Homes: Samuel going to community college, Jay and Coleman getting clean and sober. We presented data supporting our case that it was cheaper to house the chronically homeless rather than let them die on the streets or cycle through the jails and emergency rooms.

Our potential donor seemed impressed and nodded along until Dale got to the ask: $500,000.

"I love the work you do, Dale, but we can't do that," he told us. "It's almost the end of the year and we are fully committed."

The answer crushed us both. We had secretly hoped Dave would somehow answer a prayer. This property might not be there next year. We had an option to buy but not forever. We truly needed a miracle.

Nine days later my computer announced an unexpected message.

I called Dale's office immediately. "I just got an e-mail from Dave Campbell. He wants more information!"

Maybe we still had a chance. Dale and I verified all our numbers before submitting answers to his questions.

We waited nervously for a reply. A few days later, more questions arrived. We e-mailed more data and answers. A few weeks passed. Nothing.

Then one morning, Dale walked into my office. "I just got off the phone with Dave." He paused for dramatic effect. "They are sending a check for $500,000."

Dave had said the check would be in the mail, but Dale asked if we could pick it up to thank our miracle-makers in person.

November 11, 2008—almost a year exactly to the date of the first True Blessings—we walked into a conference room to receive the first check for a housing dream we didn't even have a year ago. With absolutely no fanfare, Dave Campbell graciously handed us a plain white envelope.

We felt there should have been a band playing, a full chorus singing, and confetti falling from the ceiling. To Dave, it was just another day at the office. To us, this was the moment of a lifetime. And an early Christmas miracle.

———

Every year my daughters wrote letters to Santa. Even when they were old enough to know who Santa really was, I made them write their Christmas wish lists as a letter to the North Pole.

"If you don't believe, you don't receive!" I'd tell them.

The main reason I kept insisting they write every year was because the letters were so entertaining. More than once, Kailey wrote:

Dear Santa,
    For Christmas could I please, please have:

    Baby Brother
    Pink Barbie jeep

Kailey was disappointed each Christmas when neither of these items appeared under our tree. Maddie's and Emma's lists were always suspiciously the same. I had long suspected that Maddie wrote Emma's for her, thereby doubling her own chances of receiving what she wanted.

Lauren, being the oldest, had the most experience appealing to Santa and used the most hilarious techniques. This is one of my favorites:

Dear Santa,
    This Christmas, Lauren wants:

1. To be shrunk to the size of Thumbelina
2. Muzzles to put on the twins
3. Industrial solvents
4. Cookies
5. iPod. Please give this one serious consideration

Lauren was wise enough to know I always got her at least one thing on her list, and she was betting I would go for the iPod over the industrial solvents.

In my first year as director of Homeless to Homes, I asked the residents to make a Santa wish list for Christmas 2008. This was the first Christmas in years many of them had been housed. Some, like Coleman, had spent many holidays on the streets.

Instead of going to the UMC for its annual turkey celebration, Joann and I planned a special Christmas dinner for just our tenants. Ever since we realized how lonely tenants like Raymond were, we had been working to build a community. Joann and I organized birthday lunches, picnics, and even fishing trips to a local park.

Christmas would be the first big holiday for our new family, and we wanted to make it special. We received a donation of thirteen three-foot trees, and a book club hosted an ornament-making party so the residents could create their own decorations. Everyone's apartment was made festive with purchases from the dollar store, and we promised a Santa delivery on Christmas Eve with presents from the tenants' wish lists.

As we stood in the men's department of Target, Emma and Maddie helped me sort through the thirteen letters. The tenants' lists had been achingly simple.

Socks. Underwear. A warm jacket.

"Mom, we can't just give these guys underwear!" Emma said when she saw the requests. Joann had told each resident they could ask for one "special wish," and these were the items where we could have a little more fun.

An NFL Carolina Panthers sweatshirt. A James Bond DVD. A pair of earrings.

"Mom, do you think Samuel needs XL or XXL?" Maddie asked, holding up a Panthers jersey. That was a popular wish item and we already had several in the cart.

My mom called while we were deciding.

"Hey, Mom, I'm shopping for Homeless to Homes Christmas gifts, so I can't talk right now."

"Ooh, how fun! I'll help! Let's tell your sisters and make this our family service project this year!"

As we all got older, my sisters and I didn't really need much. So each year, Louise, Allyson, Mom, and I agreed to contribute to a charity in lieu of buying gifts for each other.

"You get everyone something special from all the Green Girls," my mom said. I smiled. I had been married more than twenty years, and I was still a Green Girl.

With the extra funds from my family, we bought each resident everything on their lists plus a grocery gift card to make their own special dinner. We piled all the purchases on our dining-room table, where the twins wrapped thirteen sets of presents, careful to make each pile equal.

"Mom, I think we need to get something more for TJ and Chuck. Their piles don't look even," Maddie said.

"And Edna really got more than Ruth, so we need to go back for her too," Emma added.

Kailey made trays of Christmas cookies for each resident, and on Christmas Eve day, we caravanned in two cars loaded with four girls and presents to take to the apartments.

When we pulled up, Raymond was already waiting.

"Welcome! Welcome!" he called to my girls as we got out of the car. As we approached his apartment, we could see he had wrapped his entire front door with silver foil and taped holiday greeting cards to it. "Merry Christmas!" he called out.

"Merry Christmas, Raymond!" they said, giving him a hug as they entered his home.

"Did you see my tree?" he asked.

We all admired his small pine bending from the weight of the homemade ornaments. The tree was so small it barely came up to his waist, but to Raymond, it was better than the one in Rockefeller

Center. "Look at that!" he said, pointing at the festive display in his living room. "I can't believe it, no sir." He choked up as he spoke to my girls. "Last Christmas I was living in a barn. I am blessed," he said, wiping his eyes. "I am blessed."

That night at my home, we Izards opened one present each. It was a tradition started when Lauren and Kailey were younger and could not wait to open gifts on Christmas morning. In accordance with family tradition, we each selected one present and waited until it was our turn to unwrap as everyone watched.

"Open ours, Mom!" Kailey said, handing me a small box.

The girls gathered together in anticipation, watching as the ribbon fell to the floor and I struggled with the tape. Maddie bounced like Tigger, her nickname. She was terrible at keeping secrets, and finally it was too much.

"It's for your building, Mom!" she said.

"Maddie! Hush!" Lauren and Kailey scolded.

"Let her open it first before you tell her!" Emma cried.

Inside was $200 cash—their Christmas money from my mom. She always sent them money so they could do an Izard Girl service project for Christmas, just like the Green Girls did.

"We know you are raising money, and this won't buy a room or anything, but we figured we could buy the doorknob!" Lauren explained proudly.

I grabbed them all for a group hug. I had the Best. Family. Ever. Four days later I had the second-best Christmas gift. On December 29, 2008, the UMC became the proud owners of that junkyard beneath the cell tower. Matt Wall had made a deal with the sellers, and we closed before year's end.

It was official. We were real. We were going to build a home for homeless people.

—

Two weeks later I wanted to exchange that holiday gift of a junkyard.

During negotiations, we had factored in a low purchase price with a little reserve for the massive debris removal. The piles of rusting auto parts, however, camouflaged a much larger underground problem: barrels of oil that had been leaking into the ground for years.

The extensive cleanup was only one of our headaches that winter. We never imagined converting a junkyard to a new apartment complex would be so unpopular in the neighborhood.

Daniel Grier represented his neighborhood association, and I met with him one morning in the same diner where Joann and I held our holiday dinner with Homeless to Homes residents. I brought David Furman's construction drawings, which showed how the new three-story building would dramatically improve the rustyard of autos and trash.

I pointed out all the features I thought Daniel and the neighborhood association would appreciate: twenty-four-hour security, an art room, library, a computer lab, and gardens.

"Our members will never go for it," Daniel said. "In fact, I think they will fight it every step of the way."

I was stunned. How could he not think this is an improvement over a rusting junkyard?

Daniel carefully explained. It wasn't the building they didn't want; it was the people in it.

"But they won't be homeless anymore once they are moved in. They will be housed," I argued. "And they will have case managers to help them be just as stable or more stable than anyone else in the neighborhood."

Daniel gestured at the drawings. "You think anyone would let you put this in the wealthy neighborhoods? They only put things like this in poor neighborhoods."

Daniel knew, and I knew, he was right. This wouldn't fly in most areas of town. Charlotte was just like any city that had NIMBY attitudes—"Not in My Backyard." Philosophically, people might agree with low-income housing, but no one wanted it next door.

What Daniel hadn't realized yet was our junkyard was already properly zoned, so whether the neighborhood wanted it or not, we could build. Even so, over the weeks and months ahead, I went to meetings trying to convince people that we weren't trying to ruin the neighborhood. I had no success.

Our Homeless to Homes residents already living quietly in this same neighborhood read the unwelcome signs as well. Raymond had been at Frank's Supermarket, only blocks from our newly acquired junkyard, when a woman in front of him in the checkout line turned around to speak.

"Did you hear?" she asked him. "They're trying to move a whole building of homeless people into our neighborhood!"

Raymond just nodded, feigning his dismay.

seventeen

PAPERS AND PRAYERS

Tell me, what is it you plan to do
with your one wild and precious life?

—Mary Oliver[1]

By April 2009, the rhetoric had grown nasty. Luckily, my home phone number was unlisted, but my e-mail was distributed to the neighborhood association where we were trying to build. One member took to sending me late-night rants about her extreme opposition to our project in general and me in particular, copying the entire Charlotte City Council. One especially disturbing e-mail ended with her telling me, "You are not Jesus Christ."

I stared at my computer screen in shock. How had it come to this: people hating this cause and me? I had never set out to be a crusader. I was just trying to fulfill a promise, do some good, and "build some beds."

I found myself pushing against my quitting threshold. The

distinct probability of failure faced me: reason number one to quit. This was no longer fun and required an incredible amount of work: reason number two to quit.

I didn't want to tell anyone, including Charlie, how ugly things had become, because I was afraid they would urge me to give it up, and I didn't need any encouragement on that. My friends were already nervous for me—one even gave me a Taser for self-defense, fearing I might need it in the neighborhood.

On top of the opposition, the economy was getting worse, making the idea of raising $10 million completely unrealistic. Since that miracle $500,000 gift, no other donors had come forward in almost six months. Dale, Hugh, Downie, and I had pitched to several corporations and foundations but had no promising leads because we were not a typical civic project.

With the expenses of buying and cleaning up the lot, our funds were dwindling with no real prospects for more grants. Our best hope was Bill Holt's dream of big-bank giving, but the Wells Fargo buyout of Wachovia had made that idea much more complicated. Wells Fargo was reorganizing employees and job titles, so no one was sure who could authorize a large corporate gift.

Some of the residents were struggling as much as I was that spring. Although the pilot program was proving successful, we learned its weaknesses. Without the money to build our own building, our program had a huge flaw—we couldn't protect tenants. Facilities such as the Prince George had a security guard to monitor who came and went. The turnstiles I had seen in the lobby weren't designed to keep residents in. I now understood they were to keep dangerous people out.

Joann and I were learning that those most at risk in our apartments were women escaping violence, and those who were trying to break away from drug activity. Abusive boyfriends and drug dealers inevitably found out where our tenants were living, even if we tried to move them to different apartments. We needed twenty-four-hour security to keep tenants safe at home.

My biggest heartbreak that spring involved a resident named Christine, who had become a darling of the program. Christine was barely five feet tall and almost as round, with black hair badly dyed auburn on the ends. When we first moved her in, Christine was a teary mess of hugs for everyone, incredulous that the modest square footage belonged to her. With a bellowing laugh and a husky smoker's voice, Christine was always the rowdiest and friendliest at our Homeless to Homes community gatherings.

This same friendliness had enabled Christine to survive on the streets by attracting imposing male boyfriends to become her "protectors." Unfortunately these protectors physically abused her. Christine determined it was better to be beaten by a boyfriend than by a stranger.

When she first moved in, Christine confessed, "You don't know how glad I am to be done with that life."

Christine was a model tenant, helping cook for her neighbor next door and giving up her heavy drinking. After a few months, however, Christine started to slide back into her old habits, and we weren't sure why.

"I'm worried about her, Kathy," Joann said. "She's hiding something, and, really, she looks terrible again."

Clear-eyed Christine once more had eyes that became red-rimmed and bleary, and she often wouldn't answer the door before noon.

"She's got someone in there with her," Raymond told me. "I let her know we don't need her messing up."

After more than a year together, the thirteen residents all looked out for each other. Joann and I rarely had to enforce the apartment rules—the tenants did it themselves. Several residents had confronted Christine about the man sneaking in and out her back door.

Due to the experimental nature of the program, each tenant was afraid of making a mistake that would jeopardize everyone else's housing. We had let them know that proving Housing First could work meant helping dozens more. We all were nervous that an arrest or something similar might disrupt this effort. Most often I worried about a front-page article that would overshadow every feel-good moment of the last year. One drug bust, fight, or apartment fire might make the UMC board members vote to shut down the program.

Christine was looking like that problem.

The "someone" Raymond had identified was Christine's old street boyfriend, and he was no small problem. The first time I saw Christine's secret man, I was at the apartments looking down at my phone, unaware he was approaching me on the courtyard sidewalk. When six feet six of muscle brushed by me, I turned around to see his immense back disappearing around the corner. Our little enclave of apartments didn't get many visitors, so I was sure he was the man the other tenants had been complaining about. He was huge—terrifyingly so. I could see why no one, including Christine, was doing much about his presence.

Christine swore to us he was not living there; he was just "a friend who dropped by." Unless Christine was now wearing size 13 sneakers, the clothes in her closet told a different story.

"Can we call the police?" Dale asked in our summit about the situation.

Joann shook her head. "Not unless we can get Christine to swear out a warrant against him, and she won't."

"Should we evict her?" I asked.

"This program is about second, third, and fourth chances,"

Mom and Dad with
Maddie (L) and Emma (R), 1994

Leighton and Lindsay
Green at their wedding
rehearsal dinner, 1958

The Green Girls (L to R): me, Louise, Allyson, 1965

Izard family in Wyoming, 1997

Sarah Belk and me (front horse) on pack trip in Wind River Range, 1998

Lauren (seated), Kailey, and me at the top of Grant's Peak in Wind River Range, 1998

Urban Ministry Center with community garden in foreground, 2015

Dale Mullennix, executive director, Urban Ministry Center

Liz Clasen-Kelly, former assistant director, Urban Ministry Center, and executive director, Men's Shelter of Charlotte

(L to R) Angela Breeden, Denver Moore, and Edwina Willis Fleming at the first True Blessings, Charlotte, November 14, 2007

(L to R) Louise, me, Maddie, and Emma

Campsite where
Coleman used to live

After twenty years on the
streets, Coleman with the
keys to his new home, 2008

Eugene Coleman and Scott Mercer, Christmas 2017

Junkyard purchased as the building site for Moore Place, 2009

Moore Place courtyard, 2012

"Chilly Willy"
(William Larry Major)
at a Moore Place bingo night, 2012

Moore Place with street signage, 2016

Brothers Johnny and
Larry ("Chilly Willy") Major
in front of Moore Place, 2012

John and Pat Moore, Moore Place
Grand Opening, January 29, 2012

Bill Holt, former executive
vice president, Wells
Fargo, and current EVP,
First Tennessee Bank

Caroline Chambre Hammock, former
executive director, Moore Place

Joann said. "I want to give her the opportunity to do the right thing. But she is so afraid of him I don't think she will."

Christine didn't.

Joann called me one morning with the news. "She's gone."

I didn't need to ask. "Christine?"

"Yes, but there's more," she warned. "The appliances are gone. A truck came in the middle of the night, took them out of the kitchen along with Christine."

Not wanting to believe that Christine would do such a thing, I drove to the apartment to see for myself. The bare and damaged Sheetrock in the apartment Mark Bass entrusted to us confirmed the truth. Christine and her muscle man had forcibly removed the stove and refrigerator along with all her possessions.

I dreaded telling Mark, but he was remarkably understanding. We agreed the UMC would replace the appliances, and he was still willing to take a chance on a new tenant. With this, the best outcome, I should have been happy. But the thought of what was happening to Christine haunted me.

Was she alive? Was she dead?

Had that hulking muscleman beaten the life out of tiny Christine?

For the next few months I kept an eye out for her at the Urban Ministry Center, hoping Christine would show up in Joann's office. Maybe she would finally take out a warrant on the guy, and we could get her back into housing.

I never saw Christine again. Her disappearance was a brutal reminder that we needed our own building with twenty-four-hour security if we were ever going to provide lasting change.

Losing Christine was also when I realized I could no longer quit before achieving that goal. This job gave me all the reasons I needed to give up—it was probably going to fail, and it was too difficult. But now I had a more important reason to stay: I cared too much. The issue of homelessness was no longer abstract; it was personal.

Denver had changed me. I could no longer not see the problem. Now that I had seen, I could no longer not see. I couldn't walk into the UMC parking lot without being overcome by what had been invisible to me. I couldn't walk through that parking lot and not worry what happened after the gates closed at 4:30 p.m.

I couldn't quit because as difficult as this job was, I had learned too well it was easy compared to being homeless.

———

"I'll take the fried chicken with hush puppies and collards, corn-bread, sweet tea, and two pieces of sweet potato pie to go," Raymond said. "But just the pie to go. The rest I'll have here."

Joann looked at me and smiled. We were gathered with all the Homeless to Homes residents around a long table at the diner in our neighborhood for the monthly birthday celebration. Gigi had taught me the best way to build family was to eat together and talk together, so we now planned at least one group lunch a month. The first outing we organized had been eye opening. I realized most of our thirteen tenants had not eaten in a restaurant in years. One or two had trouble reading the menu, and the idea of sitting together at a table was incredibly awkward. The waitress had looked curiously at our unusual group of mixed ages, ethnicities, and genders. But like most southerners, she was polite.

"Can I get y'all something to drink? Honey, you want sweet or unsweet tea?"

Eventually we became regulars, and the staff greeted us warmly. They still didn't know who or what kind of group we were, but they welcomed us anyway. As we waited for our food, we would discuss local and national news stories, sports, and, of course, weather. Everyone had a TV and watched a lot of it.

"Did you see about that forest fire in California?"

"Who'd you pick for the Final Four?"

"It's going to be 97 today!"

At first, just the birthday person would get to order extra pie, but eventually, everyone ordered two pieces to go.

Our little group started to be more than members of some housing experiment. They became friends. Raymond teased Teddy, who never talked. James ribbed Ruth for talking too much. Chuck was the intellectual who read the *Wall Street Journal* and knew more about foreign affairs than I did.

Everyone lived in Mark Bass's apartment complex, except Coleman. When we housed Coleman, Mark's place was full, so we rented a unit about ten miles away. Coleman was excited about it at first because he considered it a nicer neighborhood, but eventually it became a problem.

He was lonely. Lonelier than Raymond had been. Coleman needed a friend.

The answer to his loneliness came from a church that had heard about Homeless to Homes.

"We have a group of volunteers who are trained as Stephen Ministers," the pastor explained when he called me. Stephen Ministers are church members who have not gone to divinity school but are trained to give support to their fellow congregants. "Problem is, we don't have enough people in the church who say they want help. I have all these folks wanting to give help and nobody who will say they want to receive help."

Coleman became the first tenant to be paired with a Stephen Minister.

Scott Mercer had moved to Charlotte in 1992 with his wife,

Julie, and their four children. Working full-time for a large corporate insurance company, he devoted himself to family and church. When he found his true calling, it was not during a church service but on his front porch.

Scott loved reading the morning newspaper and thought they must have the most accurate paperboy because the paper was always folded neatly on his front steps. Scott truly believed someone with perfect aim threw those papers that landed on his porch every day. One morning around 5:30 a.m., Scott noticed a figure on his lawn. Looking closer, Scott was surprised to realize it was his neighbor, Jack Merrill, an older man, stooping softly to place the paper with great care on Scott's porch before quietly moving on to the next house. Jack wasn't actually delivering the papers, Scott realized; he was just moving them from the driveway to the front door as a service to his fellow neighbors. Scott was struck by his neighbor's kindness but not surprised. Jack and his wife, Babs, were well known in the neighborhood, and kids claimed Mr. Merrill as a favorite playmate.

A few years later, when Jack developed leukemia and ended up in the hospital, Scott discovered that the paper route wasn't just a neighborhood courtesy—it was a ministry.

After learning Jack was in the hospital, Scott offered to assume the paper route—or paper placement—until his neighbor was well again. Jack was immensely thankful but admitted moving the papers to the front porches was only part of the assignment.

In order to deliver the papers correctly, Scott learned he must do something else.

"You don't just move the papers closer, Scotty," Jack told him. "You have to say a prayer for each and every family."

Scott was a little taken aback. He didn't pray for himself, much less others.

"Well, that's the gig," said Jack. "I learned this in college from one of my professors at Samford University in Birmingham. He taught me to start each day off right with a little random kindness and gratitude."

Since he had already committed to assuming the route, Scott agreed to this second, unwanted task.

It was awkward at first, but over time the morning ritual began seeping into his soul. As he delivered each paper, Scott loved the connection he felt to his neighbors and to God.

In November 2006, Jack passed away, and his obituary noted the famous paper route, calling Jack's life a "sermon in action." In tribute, Scott permanently took over the prayers and papers Jack left behind. Scott had always thought the ultimate act of service was a foreign mission trip, but this simple morning act of kindness occurring on his own street changed his mind. Maybe Scott didn't need to wait to go to a third-world country to help people. He could start right now helping people in his hometown.

As he prepared to meet Coleman, Scott didn't know what to expect. Would he and Coleman be so impossibly different they couldn't connect? How would he talk to someone who had been homeless for more than twenty years? But Scott and Coleman soon found they shared a love of sports, a commitment to people, and a passion for good food.

They met each week to attend a baseball game or to have Sunday dinner with Scott's wife and kids. It wasn't long before Coleman became part of the Mercer family.

In learning to trust Scott, Coleman shared a part of his story that few knew. It was true that Coleman had met Joann right after his encounter with the man who got cut in half by the train. But Coleman told Scott the real reason he had the courage to approach Joann was because he'd met a man who was as much of an angel as Scott.

A year before, after Coleman had prayed, "God, I don't want to die out here," he had been at the UMC getting lunch. A volunteer came up and touched the huge cyst on Coleman's shoulder. It was now as big as a small melon.

"Son, you need to do something about that."

Maybe because he had just witnessed the man killed by the train, Coleman was starting to believe this growth might actually kill him. Coleman did what he hadn't done before: he admitted his fear to this UMC volunteer.

"I can't go to a hospital again," Coleman said and confessed the whole story about the pain and paralysis from his hernia operation.

"Tell you what; how about you help me with some odd jobs, and I will help you get a surgeon who will take that thing off and do it right?"

Skeptical, Coleman agreed. But he secretly planned to miss the appointment even as the kind man promised to make one.

Coleman began meeting the man each morning to help him with odd jobs. One day after finishing early, they stopped for lunch at a fried-chicken restaurant. His new boss went to order while Coleman went into the restroom. As he was coming out, an African American woman in her fifties was standing right outside the door almost blocking his exit.

"Ma'am, this is the men's room. You don't want to come in here," he said.

"No, I know. I was waiting for you," she told him. "I have a message from God for you."

Coleman had no idea why she would say that to him, but he wanted to get away from her. He tried to move past, but he was trapped in the tight hallway.

"Go ahead, everything is going to be all right," she cryptically assured him.

Every hair on his body stood up. Did she mean the surgery? Had his new friend put her up to this?

"If you allow me," she went on, "I'm supposed to pray for you." And there, in the cramped restroom hallway of a fried-chicken chain, she put her hand on his arm, bowed her head, and prayed. By the time the prayer was over, Coleman said, he felt as if the weight of his enormous cyst lifted and he was light as a feather.

No sooner had she whispered amen than she was gone, leaving him in the hall alone and astonished. Coleman walked slowly to join his friend, who had been watching his unusual interaction.

"Who was that?" the man asked Coleman.

Coleman didn't know. He was starting to explain when the man's cell phone rang. It was the hospital. They had a cancellation and could see Coleman day after tomorrow for surgery. Could he make that?

Coleman thought of the mysterious woman, her assurances, and her prayer.

"I believe I can," Coleman said.

This time there were no complications—only one more tiny miracle. The procedure was an outpatient procedure, but in Coleman's case, because he had no home, he would be released after surgery onto the streets. Coleman worried he would die of an infection, not being able to properly care for the wound in his dirty camp under the bridge. But when it came time to leave the surgery center, Coleman was told he was going to Samaritan's House—a respite care home in Charlotte for cases like his. Coleman spent three days in Samaritan's House, and although the surgery left a scar from shoulder to shoulder, he walked out on the fourth day and never had a problem with his incision.

Ever since Coleman had prayed to a God he didn't believe in, it seemed good things had begun happening. First the stranger with work, then the prayer woman, then a successful surgery, then meeting Joann, being accepted by Homeless to Homes, getting sober, and befriending Scott Mercer.

It was enough to make a man start believing in something.

eighteen

THE FIRST YES

*When you want something, all the universe
conspires to help you achieve it.*

—Paulo Coelho[1]

I was starting to believe in something too. If I had heard Coleman's story a year earlier, the word *prayer* would have made me squirm. But that was before I met Lynn Pearce Tate or Scott Mercer or even Coleman. That was before Bill Holt had wandered into my life with the same dream of doing something about the same problem that was keeping me up at night. Not only was this project much bigger than I had imagined, I sensed it was also being designed by someone other than me.

It was time to live up to the second promise I had made Denver.

David Furman's architectural drawings were complete, but we still didn't have a name for our project. Sixteen months before, when he was leaving Charlotte, I had asked Denver, "Can I name it after you?"

At that time I didn't even know what "it" was. Now I did.

I invited John and Pat Moore to the Urban Ministry Center, telling them I wanted to give them a progress report on the pilot program. When they arrived, they brought their adult son, Kent, who was also a volunteer at the UMC. Kent sang with our homeless choir, Voices of Love.

After I gave the Moores a Homeless to Homes update, I spread the newly finished architectural rendering on the conference table. David, along with fellow architect Steve Barton, had dreamed big: three stories formed an L shape around an interior courtyard with a pavilion. Their plan showed all the features I had seen at the Prince George building in New York City: a computer lab, a library, an art center, a community garden, secured entrance, medical room, and counseling center. Natural light would fill the building through windows in every apartment, and the dining room would feature three-story glass panels soaring on two sides. There would be eighty-five studio apartments, each a modest 366 square feet, with their own galley kitchens and bathrooms.

Going through all the drawings with John and Pat, I wished they could be made real just by willing them into existence.

It was time to tell them the reason we had asked them here.

"In honor of all you have done and all Denver inspired, we would like to name this Moore Place," I told them. "After all three of you."

John looked shocked, and Pat's eyes welled up. Kent laughed. "I can't wait to see how this goes! They have never let anything be named after them!"

A minute passed and neither John nor Pat spoke. I was starting to worry they thought we wanted something from them.

"We aren't looking for more money," I assured them. "We wouldn't be this far without your belief in the pilot program. This is just a way to honor that and thank you."

They were holding hands at the conference table and tearing up looking at the drawings. I knew they were private people; maybe this wasn't the honor we thought it was going to be.

Pat finally spoke, "I think if it is to honor Denver, too, then we could be all right with that."

Moore Place was fully born.

Denver Moore, John and Pat Moore. They were from different states, opposite ends of the economic spectrum, no relation, but they shared the same vision and the same last name.

Coincidence?

I was starting to believe it was something more: a God-instance.

With the building name decided, our last hurdle remained: the money. Dale and I approached large churches and existing donors, but we were greeted mostly with skepticism that we could ever raise the remaining $9.5 million. Hugh McColl III and I went on dozens of corporate and foundation calls but were met with southern politeness when we said we had exactly one funder to date backing the building project.

Applying to the city and state for money wasn't going any better. The City of Charlotte denied our request for $500,000 because the neighborhood opposed us. The neighborhood association and their city-council representative still wanted Moore Place anywhere but in their backyard.

There was a long application process for city money, which required a city council vote. At that point we had only two of the eleven representatives willing to vote for us. The state of North Carolina was even more complicated, with a request for funding requiring a lengthy legislative process. We needed money now. The amount we needed was also so huge that even a generous gift of $25,000 still left a monumental money mountain to climb. We needed big, million-dollar kinds of believers—those willing to be a little unconventional in their giving.

Bill Holt had not stopped dreaming of asking his bank, now Wells Fargo, to be such a believer. Despite the merger and the gloom caused by all the banking turmoil, Bill called periodically with optimistic updates, but meetings were inevitably dashed and further delayed by the practical realities of the merger.

None of that bothered Bill. He had faith that if we were patient, it would all work out. From the announcement of the merger in October 2008, Bill and others continued to work behind the scenes. But time was running out to realize this dream of a huge gift from a bank. No other donors were going to take us seriously if all we had was the money to buy the land.

Finally our wait ended. In March 2009, Wells Fargo named its Eastern Region President, who would decide our fate.

Bill called to give us the news: Laura Schulte had received the job. A quick Google search indicated we might have a glimmer of hope. Laura was moving from California, and one of the charities she had been involved with there was LAMP—an organization that provided housing for homeless in Los Angeles.

Further reading led to more hope. LAMP was the organization profiled in Steve Lopez's book *The Soloist,* which had been made into a movie. *The Soloist* is the true story of Nathaniel Ayers, a talented musician with schizophrenia who became homeless but was eventually housed in a LAMP apartment. We had just booked Steve Lopez to be the speaker at our next True Blessings luncheon, now going on its third year as a fundraising event for the UMC.

If nothing else, Laura Schulte would be familiar with our cause, and we could connect through the fact that Steve Lopez was coming to Charlotte on our behalf.

Twice we geared up for a presentation, and twice we were postponed due to Laura's hectic schedule. The meeting was finally set for April 15, 2009.

Dale, Bill Holt, and I rode the elevator up to the top floor of the executive offices. All of Charlotte was visible through floor-to-ceiling windows in the sky-high conference room. I thought of all the decisions that had been made in that room and wondered if any were as personal as this. Laura Schulte had no idea how momentous this day was for us. She had no idea we had done this presentation dozens of times, waiting for someone to say yes.

We started our pitch with Bill giving the background about Moore Place and Dale giving the history of the UMC, along with the Steve Lopez connection. My part was to ask for money—the crazy $3 million part.

As Bill and Dale were talking, I tried to push down the panic. When it was my turn, I started with the remarkable success of the pilot program and our dream to expand this solution to help more than thirteen people. I heard myself make the most preposterous request: "We'd like to ask Wells Fargo to partner with us, and we ask for a gift of $3 million."

I waited.

The words hung in the room. I wanted to take them back.

Say anything, I pleaded in my head, *just don't say no.*

A friend trained in fundraising had taught me that when you ask for money, any answer but no is a win. If you ask for $100,000 and you get $100, that is still a win. We needed a win. We needed something from Wells Fargo.

Laura started speaking, but I had no idea what she was saying. My head was fuzzy, and I felt nauseated with desperation. I tried to focus. She was smiling. She was nodding. She was consulting her team.

What was she saying? "Yes."

Laura Schulte said yes to $3 million for the most unlikely of projects. She said yes to chronically homeless men and women.

She said yes, and not because she thought these homeless people would become future bank customers opening accounts. She was not saying yes because this decision would improve Wells Fargo's bottom line.

I finally could hear Laura Schulte, who was saying yes because "this is the right thing to do."

She stood. We all stood. She left the room. Just like that.

Our fairy godmother left the room and had no idea that in granting our wish she had changed everything. I am sure she went on that day to make a hundred other decisions. But in our world, this was the only one that mattered. There was nothing bigger.

We filed out of the conference room and pushed the button to the elevator. Bill, Dale, and I exchanged glances, making a silent pact to wait until the elevator doors closed. We stood nonchalantly as the doors slowly came together.

Like we get $3 million commitments every day.

When the doors finally glided closed, we collapsed with relief, with happiness, and with the unimaginable improbability of it all. Even with his solid belief in God, Dale had not seen this coming. I started to cry and looked at Bill and realized he was crying too. Here was the man who had predicted it. It had been 459 days since Liz Clasen-Kelly and I sat in his office and heard his plan to ask for $3 million from his employer. At the time it was just an audacious dream, and we had all just been witness to it coming true.

We landed in the lobby as if we had just left Oz and ended up back in Kansas. I wanted to tell everyone, to call the newspaper and make it the morning's headline. But we couldn't. That was part of the deal. We had agreed to fill out grant applications, undergo a full review, and structure the terms. Wells Fargo people needed to talk with Wachovia Foundation people—a step that would turn out to be way more complicated than any of us imagined. It would take months, but that day marked our rise out of a fundraising hole.

I didn't tell anyone our news, except Charlie. Trying to recall the details of my remarkable meeting that day, I found it all hard to believe. At dinner he kindly listened to my excitement, letting it all sink in. "That's great, Kathy," he said between bites. "I'm really proud of you all."

His reaction was a little muted, and I started to wonder why.

Charlie was in finance, so even as I was telling my fantastic story, he couldn't help beginning to do the math in his head. As amazing as this news was, he immediately grasped a harsher reality. He just didn't want to be the one to tell me.

It was about an hour after we finished dinner before it hit me. We were in our den watching TV when a slow panic broke through my euphoria.

We now had $3.5 million pledged.

Pledged.

Not in the bank.

That left $6.5 million still to go. For homeless people. In a recession. In a banking city where everyone worked in the two big banks, and everyone was losing or had already lost their jobs. And everyone owned bank stocks in those same two companies where stock prices had plummeted to single digits in a matter of months.

It finally hit me, and I spoke out loud the very problem Charlie had been too nice to point out at dinner. "Where are we going to get $6.5 million?"

The miracle that was the Wells Fargo gift morphed into an insurmountable mountain. Without the other $6.5 million we couldn't pay for Moore Place, and we certainly couldn't build something we couldn't pay for.

A silence settled between us. The TV carried on oblivious to my distress. Finally I spoke my worst fear, the one that was boring silently through me, out loud: "Charlie, if we don't raise this money, does it mean I failed?"

"Kathy, if you all can raise that money in this economy it will be a miracle."

nineteen

CRAZY OR CALLED

How precious did that grace appear, the hour I first believed.

—"Amazing Grace"[1]

With the Wells Fargo pledge of $3 million and Charlie providing forgiveness from failure, I woke up each day and kept moving. But, really, I had been only a year and a half on the job, and I was exhausted. At night I counted tenants instead of sheep, and in the day I struggled to keep the girls, grant applications, and Homeless to Homes issues straight.

I tried to hide my doubts and weariness from everyone, especially Dale. He had been doing this for fifteen years. How could I complain after not even two years on the job?

Dale had calm confidence everything would work out. God would provide. I let Dale think that, but I certainly didn't believe that. My sister Louise sided with Dale. Ever since our initial conversation about Roseanne Haggarty, Common Ground, and the Prince George, my sister had an innate belief this was all going to happen.

Both Dale and Louise had faith. I didn't.

I figured the only way to get this done was the earthly way of working hard, not relying on divine intervention. I had no faith God was going to rescue us. God certainly didn't know we had a capital campaign that was short $6.5 million, that success or failure was resting squarely on me. I might agree there had been some little God-instances and even two tiny miracles with the two big gifts, but we had so far to go. I wasn't expecting God to finish it for me.

What really bothered me was that this whole thing had started when I listened to Denver, who beyond all logic compelled me to build beds. What if his voice was no different from those that used to plague my mom?

———

I have indelible memories of visiting Mom on locked psychiatric wards. The most dramatic one occurred when I was a senior in high school and Mom wouldn't open her hospital room door for my father and me to come inside.

"Lindsay," my dad implored, "please open the door. I brought Kathy, and we want to see you."

After a long, slow scraping noise, the door cracked open, and a hollow-eyed version of my mother appeared in the two-inch gap. She eyed us suspiciously, with no real sign of affection or recognition, just a slightly wild look of confusion as she whispered, "Come in, but keep your voices down."

I didn't dare look at my father. It was all too bizarre.

My mom moved back to the hospital bed, picking up her pile of index cards and the four-color Bic pen. With the multicolor pen she could record her brainstorms in the same vivid Peter Max versions that must have appeared in her head. Her attention went to the corner of the room, and her hands were poised as if ready to take dictation. She looked up expectantly at the TV, obviously entranced by the programming.

The program that held her captive on TV was *All in the Family*, a seventies hit sitcom. Archie, the main character, was legendary for his crass, unenlightened opinions. That my mother, a brilliant, well-read artist, was hanging on his every syllable for secret coded wisdom was more than a little crazy.

We didn't even try to dissuade her. There was no point. We watched the show with her and did not comment as she dutifully penned notes on her three-by-five-inch cards during commercial breaks. I guess we thought it was the least we could do to offer some quiet companionship amid the loneliness of her delusion.

We remained quiet even when the ads were on. Finally, when the episode was over, we left in silence, getting back on the elevator and walking wordlessly to our car. Dad started toward our destination, a grand-opening party for a new restaurant. My dad had done the owners' legal work, and I was going to be his date. It now seemed absurd to attend, given the scene we had just witnessed.

I broke the hush first. "Dad? Mom thinks Archie Bunker is talking to her."

The lunacy of that statement hung between us in the front seat for a few minutes.

"I know . . ." he started, but Dad seemed unable to find the encouragement or explanation he needed to comfort his seventeen-year-old daughter.

And then he did something he rarely did. He burst out laughing. There was no explaining it, but I joined him. It was the kind of silent laughter that makes you shake though no sound escapes, but your whole body gets the most wondrous release. It went on for a few minutes, like a long hug that neither of us would release. My dad was laughing so hard that tears leaked from the corners of his sad blue eyes. He wiped them away slowly, making squeaky sounds as the laughter subsided and he caught his breath. We didn't say anything else. There was nothing to say.

We went on to the party at the restaurant, and when someone asked how he was, my dad smiled convincingly and replied, "Fine. How are you?"

———

I knew when someone suffered from mental illness, it took every ounce of his or her will to keep crazy at bay. Mom's daily courage was her constant choice to live. Not only did my mom have to fight to stay sane, we had to fight to stay sane with her. If my dad had left or my grandparents had not helped me and my sisters, all of our lives would have been very different.

Having lived my mom's story, it was easy for me to feel tied to each Homeless to Homes resident, to feel personally responsible to do something about their plights. A part of me had always wanted to be the one to save my mom from her pain. But as a six-year-old or even a seventeen-year-old, there was nothing I could do. Only doctors could find the right pharmaceutical combination to restore her to the woman who would eventually pursue her master's degree and travel to China.

Yet her manic episodes made me afraid to admit my real terror now. If I was "listening" to a man who was thirty years homeless "call" me to this quest, was I any different than my mom?

Was I, at the age of forty-four, finally exhibiting the very inheritable trait for manic depression? Was Denver for real? Was any of it real?

Just as I had my whole life, I hid my fear of a nervous breakdown in the same box I hid my mom's mental illness. I never talked about it. I didn't want to tell Charlie or anyone that I was beginning to crack.

Finally, in late April, I sent an e-mail to a minister at the new church we had been attending, Christ Episcopal Church. I already knew one of the ministers, Lisa Saunders, because Kailey and her daughter had played soccer together. I e-mailed Lisa, asking if she would meet with me. I had no idea what I would say, but I had to talk with someone who was not a part of the Moore Place story so I could be honest. I had to tell someone: I think I'm truly crazy.

—

As I drove to the appointment with the minister, I wrestled with what I would say. Was I mentally ill or was this some sort of spiritual call?

I honestly didn't want either one. Bipolar or called—both seemed like the same kind of crazy to me.

Lisa greeted me in the church lobby and we walked back to her office, exchanging small talk. The collar around her neck was a little startling as I realized she had a professional life that was not visible on the soccer sidelines. She sat next to me in one of the two chairs that faced her desk and waited patiently as I fumbled with how to begin. My voice was catching on my doubt as I tried to explain why I was there.

I started by telling her a little about my mom's struggles with manic depression, then I outlined the overwhelming magnitude of the Moore Place master plan. It had gone from an exciting change of career to a boulder that was crushing me. As I continued to explain the resistance from neighbors, the politics, and the money challenges, she listened quietly like a therapist, knowing I would eventually see my own circle.

Finally she led me to it by asking, "So why are you here?"

Months of lying awake at night came sharply into focus. The question I had been wrestling with, refusing to address, was suddenly right before me and undeniable. I looked at her, afraid to speak, but she seemed to know what I was going to say.

"The problem is, I really want to do this," I began. "I really want to build this building."

She nodded in encouragement.

"But I am not big enough to do it myself," I finally finished.

My voice was halting, and I was trying not to cry. I had always been able to accomplish the things I truly wanted. My childhood had taught me to be pathologically self-reliant—to work hard and achieve my goals without anyone's help.

"To do this, I need to believe in something bigger than myself," I said, as if that was a huge problem. When I said it to a minister, it certainly did not seem like a problem. I tried to elaborate. "If I am going to succeed, I am going to have to believe that something besides me, bigger than me, is going to get this done."

There, I had said it. Out loud. Almost. I had avoided the G word. Lisa smiled at me. She was leaning forward, forearms on her thighs, hands together almost in prayer. "And what scares you about that?"

"Because it feels crazy! I feel like I am crazy! To believe that I have been given some message, some call, to build this thing feels crazy!" Now I was crying. "And to actually listen to it feels even crazier."

Visions of my mom and the voices she heard during my childhood were plaguing me. Wasn't I just admitting that I was in some form of a manic state, hearing voices of grand plans?

"And what if it is not?" Lisa asked simply.

What if?

What if I really was supposed to meet Denver and he really had given me a message I was supposed to hear?

What if I really was supposed to get Moore Place built?

It felt too much like a Noah kind of foolishness, but that was the heart of it.

"It is what I keep coming back to: To get this done, I have to believe in God because I can't do this myself. But to believe in God means I have to believe I got some kind of message that started this whole thing. And I can't believe that part."

"Why not?" Lisa asked.

"Why me?" I choked. "Why would someone who doesn't even believe in God get a message from God?"

"Why not you?" she responded matter-of-factly.

Because I didn't want it. Because I didn't believe that kind of thing—Dale and Louise did. I didn't even like the spiritual parts of Ron and Denver's book; when it got too preachy, prayerful, or heavenly, I had skipped those pages.

I liked reality. I believed in reality. It was fine for Denver to believe he had a prayer chain going, but not for me. How could I believe that Denver, who seemed to speak from an otherworldly place, had an otherworldly message for me?

But I was back in that circle again.

I wanted Moore Place. I didn't want to fail. But to succeed, I had to ask for help. Big help. Otherworldly kind of help. As Charlie had so clearly pointed out, it was going to take a miracle.

My immense doubt sat heavily in the room, and Lisa waited patiently to see what I would do with it.

"So how will I know?" I whispered, afraid someone, even a minister, might hear me even thinking of *believing*.

How would I know I wasn't hearing manic voices but some kind of real deal? And the really crazy thing was, my mom never stopped being a big believer. Since those college days of reading the Bible with my father, church and prayer had been a huge part of her life. Faith was truly her salvation in her darkest days.

Lisa leaned back and smiled. She seemed relaxed, like she had been waiting to deliver this punch line. "You will know," she said with utter confidence. "God has a funny way of showing off."

twenty

GIFTS FROM ABOVE

We must be willing to get rid of the life we've planned,
so as to have the life that is waiting for us.

—Joseph Campbell[1]

Leaving Lisa's office that day, I was comforted but not fully convinced.

It felt good to have finally spoken about the demon that was chasing me—I might have bipolar disorder. I decided after reflecting that it was preferable to think I was slightly manic than to believe I had been divinely chosen for this task.

Lisa's conviction stuck with me, though, and I started to sleep a little better by trying an awkward prayer as I lay down at night. I felt a little like Scott Mercer trying to pray for neighbors on his paper route. It didn't really count as prayer in the beginning. After I got in bed, I would try to release thoughts. More a list than a litany.

God, help us find some donors.

God, help the neighborhood not hate us so much.

God, help me fill out that CHA grant application.

That last plea, about the Charlotte Housing Authority grant application, was my next biggest worry. It could be worth $1.7 million of grant money and, even more critical, ongoing assistance for thirty years in rent subsidies from the federal government.

We were not excited about asking for federal money. Dale had been operating the UMC for years without taking a dime of public money—on purpose. Dale liked to act compassionately and quickly on behalf of the Neighbors. Government money meant red tape and regulations about who you could and couldn't help, so we wanted our plan to build Moore Place to rely heavily on churches and individuals.

Once it was built, however, we needed government partnership. If we could partner with the CHA to provide federal rental subsidies, called Section 8 vouchers, homeless people could move in directly off the streets and work with Moore Place social workers to apply for income from disability payments. No longer sleep deprived and in a housing crisis, our tenants could make completely different decisions about their addictions, education, and life. Just as Coleman, Samuel, and Raymond had done.

It would change everything for almost a hundred people, not just thirteen.

But this crucial partnership with the CHA and the federal government had a huge hurdle I had not been able to clear. The incredibly complicated federal application entailed completing binders full of information and providing detailed budget projections for the next thirty years.

As I leafed through the dense list of requirements, I was clearly in trouble. This was not about me wanting to do good. This was real business. I needed an MBA, not a graphics degree.

One day as I worked my way through the lunch crowd of Neighbors at the UMC, trying to get to Dale's office to confess I had no idea how we'd ever complete the grant application, I was stopped by Jerry Licari. Jerry had been in the car that day when we first spotted the junkyard lot and had been waiting for a task on this project ever since. I hadn't given him one because I wasn't sure what to ask him to do. He was Dale's pick for the team, and I didn't know what Jerry's skills were.

"Excited to hear about all the progress on Moore Place," he said as I tried to pass him. "I'd love to be doing more; is there anything I can do to help?"

My sarcasm escaped before I could stop it. "Not unless you can do proformas."

I knew so little about the term that I didn't even know if I had expressed my need correctly.

He looked at me strangely. "Are you kidding?"

I locked eyes with him and got a weird feeling. "No, why?"

"I love that stuff!" he exclaimed and started laughing. "I'm a retired partner from a Big Eight accounting firm. I can do that in my sleep."

I tried not to burst into tears.

As it turned out, Jerry was a financial wizard who became the volunteer chief financial officer for Moore Place. We would be joined at the hip for the next year and a half. He created and endlessly revised financials for Moore Place. We attended countless meetings together and worked for months to craft the documents needed to secure public funding.

When the CHA held a vote on whether to award Moore Place $1.7 million in construction funds and thirty years' worth of Section 8 rental subsidies, Jerry was sitting right beside me. Together, we watched the CHA board members raise their hands one by one and vote yes.

What I didn't know until almost four years later is how improbable that meeting with Jerry turned out to be. We were having coffee in 2013, when Jerry confessed that the day we spoke at the UMC was the first time he had admitted his accounting background. After retiring in 2006, he had made a pledge to himself to do something completely different with his life. He was done with the accounting world; he wanted no part of it.

Jerry had researched nonprofit agencies before his retirement, selecting the UMC as one of two he wanted to serve, but he only wanted to be a counselor. When the UMC volunteer coordinator asked about his former profession, he replied, "I was a businessman." Even when Dale asked him to be on the UMC board, Jerry had not mentioned his vast accounting experience.

Jerry later confided, "That day was the first time I had told anyone at the Urban Ministry Center what I used to do for a living."

God has a funny way of showing off.

———

I looked at my watch and saw it was my table-wiping time. Every staff member, no matter his or her job description, had to clean tables in the lunchroom once a week. Dale felt it was too easy to get caught up in administrative tasks and forget why we were all there—to help our Neighbors. Something about wiping up dozens of vegetable soup spills once a week kept a person humble. But inevitably, like today, I did not want to go to the lunchroom. I really needed to finish an important grant application for the John S. and James L. Knight Foundation. We were applying for $1 million, and the deadline was looming. With the CHA vote of $1.7 million, we still needed $4.8 million to magically appear.

I had six days to submit the application, a complex matrix of exacting questions and measurements designed to confirm we knew what we were doing. It felt like I was writing a master's thesis, and in some ways I was. My effort was the culmination of a year and a half of on-the-job training and learning from other national programs. The Knight Foundation, as others, didn't care if we were doing good; they needed to be sure we could do it well. Budget projections, staffing models, and funding plans all had to be submitted along with answers to more probing questions regarding specific outcomes and expected results.

The grant would have to wait until after table duty. The lunch-room was noisy and crowded as usual. I worked my way to the back to pick up a rag and waved across the room to Liz Clasen-Kelly, who had duty that day too. As I started wiping down, I saw a young guy with wild dreadlocks get up from his table and sneak up behind those patiently waiting to pick up their trays at the stainless-steel counter. I looked back at his place where he had obviously eaten one lunch already. The UMC offered seconds on food but only in the last fifteen minutes of the lunch hour to be sure everyone was served at least once. It wasn't a crime really, and I knew everyone who came here was legitimately hungry. But he was breaking an unwritten rule that everyone else abided by. I moved up behind him to see that, sure enough, he was grabbing an extra bowlful of soup.

"Excuse me?" I said.

He looked at me, his hazel eyes wild and red-rimmed. "What?" he replied roughly.

"We aren't serving seconds yet."

"This ain't seconds," he said.

"Really?" I said, pointing to his first empty lunch plate still on the table behind us.

"What's it to you?" he asked loudly. Several people looked up, including Bill, the quiet cowboy in his dirty leather hat eating silently next to the man's empty tray.

I wasn't sure I was going to do or say anything more, but before I had the chance to decide, the soup stealer threw the offending bowl of tomatoes and noodles on me. Immediately Bill jumped up between the soup thrower and me.

"Hey! You watch yourself!" he yelled to the young rule breaker. The wild-dreadlock guy looked as though he might go after my chivalrous cowboy friend, but two other men stood up and joined Bill.

"You go on now, boy," one of them said loudly.

When the young guy turned to slink away, Bill asked, "You okay, ma'am?" He looked at me with his kind, sky-blue eyes and a weathered face as tanned and lined as his hat. He wasn't much taller than me, and I was even more surprised that he had stood up to defend me from the much larger thug.

I looked down at my blouse. Luckily most of the soup had missed me and gone on the floor.

"Yes, thanks so much. I'll be fine."

Wiping my blouse, I realized I didn't even know Bill's last name. "I really appreciate that you stood up for me. Your name is Bill?"

"Yes, ma'am. Bill, Bill Halsey," he said, tipping his hat and returning to his lunch.

Liz had been working her way through the crowd. "You okay?"

"Yes, thanks to Bill."

"Oh, I just love him," Liz said. "He's one of my favorites." She, of course, knew his story and filled me in.

Bill Halsey had one of the most unusual living arrangements of any street person in Charlotte. He had tried living in the men's shelter but it was too chaotic for him, so Bill created the only house he could. Along the railroad tracks, he had found a concrete platform that once was used to unload bales of cotton from freight cars. Bill didn't pitch a tent on top of it; he dug a hole under the concrete. It took him two months to excavate his underground home: an eight-by-eight-foot dirt cave with just enough room to stand up in. Bill had been living in that hole for about five years.

As unusual as that living arrangement sounded, I kind of understood it. Bill's need to go underground for safety was not much different from a six-year-old making a haven out of a closet's top shelf.

"My dream day," Liz said, "will be to see Chilly Willy and Bill Halsey move into Moore Place."

I finished my shift and went back to my office.

It was astounding to think someone as sweet as Bill Halsey was living in a hole in the ground. It was amazing to think men like Coleman and Samuel had been on the streets for decades. They were the faces of this argument for housing.

I had a lot of facts and data to put into the Knight application, but I also had these real-life stories that told why it truly mattered. Would someone at the Knight Foundation care about an argument of the heart as much as an argument designed for the head? I took a chance in the closing section. Maybe it was more appropriate to stick with formal technical language and statistics. But maybe, just maybe, those reviewing the applications got tired of reading all that and wanted to hear what truly mattered:

One fifty-year-old resident named Samuel, who was in our pilot program, was visiting the UMC after his first day of classes at the local community college. He was impeccably groomed and dressed in a pressed collared shirt and proudly held his college backpack.

He stood out amid the tattered crowd of four hundred gathered in line for the UMC Soup Kitchen lunchtime meal. He had previously been a part of that crowd for more than twenty years. As he showed others his syllabus and books, a UMC employee marveled, "I can't believe it. I always thought he was a lost cause."

He and twelve others are proving daily in Charlotte that there are no lost causes. Moore Place will offer the possibility of transformation to eighty-five others. Their collective chance for change will offer inspiration and hope not only to those seeking housing but more importantly, to the housed among us who once believed the homeless were hopeless.

I sent up a little prayer as I pressed send.

———

Although we were focused on fundraising, the resistance from the neighborhood association around our junkyard had not gone away. Throughout that summer we attended city and neighborhood meetings, trying to change sentiment, but it wasn't working.

In late July 2009, I checked my e-mail and couldn't believe what I was reading. It was a message from a church in the neighborhood that wanted to help:

> [We] recently heard that the property across the street from us has been purchased by the Urban Ministry Center. We are thrilled about that and hope we can partner with whatever is going on there in the future.

I knew the church because it was directly across the street from our junkyard purchase. It didn't look like a traditional church—just a simple cement building that I had driven past a hundred times. It felt almost too good to be true—a friend in the neighborhood? A group of people who claimed to be thrilled we were building there?

It was a hot southern summer day when I showed up at the church, but I was sweating for other reasons. I needed this to go well. After all the neighborhood meetings where people had been unpleasant, even hostile, I worried I was being set up for confrontation.

As promised, however, it was just the pastor and two friendly church members who greeted me. We sat down awkwardly in kid-sized chairs in a classroom. The happy sounds of a children's summer Bible camp spilled in from the room next door. After exchanging introductions, I brought out our brochures with the drawings of Moore Place in hopes of convincing them they had nothing to fear or protest. I was desperate to assure this congregation that their new neighbors would be like Coleman—good people who needed a chance.

"You don't need to convince us," the pastor said. "We already want to help. We did an all-church read of a book and it was very powerful."

I was amazed—an entire congregation wanting to work together on homelessness? It was a small church with seemingly limited resources, so I was even more impressed that they wanted to give back so generously.

"Wow—that's great," I said. "What was the book?"

"*Same Kind of Different As Me*," he replied.

Of course it was.

Both Dale and my sister Louise laughed when I told them.

"Kathy, you cannot make this up!" Louise said over the phone. "You are on some kind of cosmic journey! You better start writing all this down!"

I sent Lisa Saunders a simple e-mail that night: **God showed off again today.**

—

Once I was looking and listening, it seemed God was everywhere.

I had not talked to Scott Mercer much since we had paired him with Coleman, but we needed more help raising money. With a vested interest in one of our Homeless to Homes residents, I hoped Scott might be willing to be on the team asking for corporate and private donations. We met at a pancake house and talked so much about Coleman and their friendship, we barely got around to the Moore Place Capital Campaign.

"Coleman had dinner at our house a couple of months ago, and I served him some of my special BBQ sauce," Scott told me.

"'Scott, this is so good you should sell it,' Coleman told me. And so we are!" Scott announced.

He proudly showed me a photo of the new joint venture with Coleman. A red, white, and blue bottle of BBQ sauce with the label reading, "EC's Home BBQ Sauce—The taste that brings you home."

They had already started bottling and were looking for retailers to carry their product. Scott told me the kicker. "Coleman wants to give the proceeds to the Urban Ministry Center for all they've done for him."

Scott confided he believed he was destined to meet Coleman. They'd formed a family bond much like Denver Moore and Ron Hall's.

We were talking so much that I almost forgot why I had asked Scott to meet. As he was hurrying out, I put a Moore Place brochure in Scott's hands and asked if he would help raise money. The brochure had been created by two of my advertising friends, Julie Marr and Arkon Stewart. The pages featured three people—a doctor, Jane Harrell, telling the story of how housing was vital to health; a district attorney, telling the story of how housing prevented misuse of community tax dollars; and Coleman, telling his story of the transformative power of housing.

Scott quickly flipped through the pages and agreed to connect later on the details. That afternoon, I opened this e-mail from Scott:

Kathy,

You are never going to believe this. When we were looking at the brochure this morning, I missed a page and testimonial from my physician, Dr. Jane Harrell. We have a special connection because due to her intuition and diligence, she diagnosed me with early stage prostate cancer. At my fairly youthful age (by medical standards), most patients my age would not have been screened. In effect, Dr. Harrell saved me from a much worse outcome. The truth be known, I will always credit Dr. Harrell with saving my life. We have talked about this openly, and we have talked about my "paper route," and she feels strongly that she was guided to have me screened for a greater purpose in my life.

You should have seen my face when I looked through the brochure again this morning upon returning to my office from our breakfast and seeing Dr. Harrell's testimonial just one page behind Coleman's. It really gave me chills. I can't wait to share with Jane on my next checkup. She will be blown away when she finds out that I was paired with Coleman in your program!

Scotty

It was beyond coincidence. I hadn't even known Dr. Jane Harrell when we put her in the brochure. She was helping start a clinic at the UMC, and Dale had suggested she present the medical perspective in our brochure. Neither of us knew she had any connection to Scott Mercer or Coleman.

I could no longer be surprised working on this project. Now, anytime there was a God-instance, I just looked straight up and whispered thank you.

———

It was September 14, 2009. I had been watching the calendar all month and the clock all day. Susan Patterson with the Knight Foundation had told me the vote would be today. Our campaign was stuck at just under $6 million, and we needed a boost. The million dollars they were voting on would not only push us past the critical halfway mark but also signal to other foundations and donors that we were legitimate. All of the work on that master's thesis of an application came down to today.

I stared at the phone on my desk, willing it to ring. Willing it to bring good news.

When it did ring, I was afraid to answer because a no would be too devastating.

"Kathy, they voted," Susan began. I could imagine her bright red hair and stylish black glasses.

"The John S. and James L. Knight Foundation is pleased to award Moore Place a grant of $1 million."

Relief overwhelmed me. It seemed that heart-and-head argument I had written had worked. All the meetings, all the cups of coffee, and the grant requests were finally starting to pay off. We now had $6,997,000 of the $10 million we needed. Susan suggested we hold a press conference to announce how far we had come and ask the public to help us raise the final $3 million.

We were already excited about announcing our success to date when the senior pastor at Scott Mercer's church—Myers Park Presbyterian—telephoned Dale. The church wanted to contribute in a big way and reveal it during the live press conference, Monday, October 19, 2009. Dale added him to the program.

That morning I helped set up one hundred chairs in the old train depot. We had no idea if anyone would come, but friends and donors started arriving a little before 10:00 a.m., easily filling the room. The depot was buzzing with excitement when Jane Harrell, Scott's life-saving doctor pictured in our fundraising brochure, hurried over to me. Her wispy blond hair was pulled back, and under her coat she wore her blue physician's scrubs, having just come from a free clinic for the UMC. I assumed she was coming for the press conference.

"Don't think I'm crazy," she began. "I just can't sleep. God keeps telling me to do this so now I'm doing it."

With that, Jane shoved a plain white envelope in my hand, turned around, and disappeared out the door. Confused by what all that meant, I watched Jane as she headed to her car. Although I was incredibly curious about her message to me, the press conference was about to begin, so I slipped the envelope into my pocket for later.

By the time we got started, the train depot was overflowing—standing room only. The program began with Coleman and Scott each sharing a little about how they met and what a difference they had made in each other's life. Next up were representatives from Wells Fargo and the Charlotte Housing Authority. Then Dale introduced Steve Eason, the pastor from Scott's church.

With an impassioned speech, Steve spoke as if giving a Sunday morning sermon, not a press conference. His plea was powerful, but Reverend Eason's final line was the most compelling, addressing all that Charlotte had lost in the past few years due to the failing economy and the loss of the two big banks as our civic centerpieces. "We can live in a community that has lost jobs or even lost businesses," he said, "but we can't live in a community that has lost compassion."

His big finish was a surprise announcement. Myers Park Presbyterian Church was giving $250,000 to the Moore Place campaign—part of it as a challenge grant encouraging other churches to give. The church would give us $150,000 up front, and $100,000 more if fifty other churches gave something as well. Reverend Eason was calling upon the faith community to collectively declare that the homeless were worthy of support.

It was out-of-the-box thinking that a church would give such a large gift—and recruit fifty other houses of faith to join this campaign. My heart pounded as I did the math in my head: we were now almost at $7.25 million—under $3 million to go. Everyone in the room seemed to know this was huge news.

It was the best kind of feel-good story, one that would make the news on all four local stations and the front page of the newspaper the next day.

Leaving the press conference, I was ecstatic. This impossible dream was within reach.

Reaching into my coat pocket for my car keys, I found Jane's envelope. Remembering her words, I wondered what God had kept telling her to do and ripped open her envelope. There was no note, no explanation.

Just a check to Moore Place for $10,000.

twenty-one

BLESS AND MULTIPLY THIS SMALL AMOUNT

Sometimes beautiful things come into our lives out of
nowhere. We can't always understand them, but we have
to trust in them. I know you want to question everything,
but sometimes it pays to just have a little faith.

—Lauren Kate[1]

Jane Harrell's check was one of many gifts that seemed to drop from
heaven that autumn.

The good press coverage gave us a huge boost. Gifts came in
all sizes, from a children's lemonade stand that raised $105 to yet
another check for $10,000 from a woman I'd never met. She offered
no explanation of who she was or why she sent it.

By far the most mysterious gift, however, came from someone I
began calling our Mailbox Angel.

Her first gift arrived when I was checking for mail at the UMC desk, which is a Grand Central Station kind of operation. Hundreds of Charlotte's homeless people use 945 North College Street, our address, as their place of residence to receive checks or communicate with family. Thousands of letters are sorted each week by volunteers and put into cardboard boxes labeled A–B, C–D, E–H, and so on.

Staff mail arrives at the center with this landslide of communication. Oftentimes a volunteer, not recognizing Izard as an employee, would put my mail in the Neighbors' box. Because of this common occurrence, I made a habit of not only checking my staff slot in the back but also sorting through the big box of Neighbors' mail. Sure enough, one day I found a pastel envelope with my name on it that did look like a Neighbor letter from home resting in the I–L box.

I took it back to my office and turned it over. There was a return address in Charlotte but no identified sender. Just my name and the UMC address on a small pink envelope. Tearing it open, I found a greeting card inside, like one a grandmother would buy: soft colors and pictures of violets. My mother would never buy this kind. She routinely went for the Peanuts and humor cards. When I opened the card, the mystery deepened when a $10 bill fell out. Under the preprinted message was this handwritten note:

May God Bless and Multiply this small amount.

That was it. No signature. No clue.

The next month another pastel envelope arrived. Again there was no name with the return address. Just a card, a $5 bill, and the message:

May God Bless and Multiply this small amount.

The next month, another. Someone liked Hallmark as much as my mom. Each card held a different amount but the same blessing of the gift.

I started to profile my benevolent giver. A woman, I was certain. I imagined soft gray hair framing the face of an elderly, Oprah-like saint who saved up her spare dollar bills each month to send to us. I wanted to meet her and tell her that her gift gave me outsized hope each time an envelope arrived. The idea that someone I had never met would give to our cause in this way made me feel I wasn't crazy to dream this at all. Maybe a higher power was spreading the message far more convincingly than Dale and I ever could.

It seemed our Mailbox Angel's prayer was taking hold—the small amounts were being multiplied, and they were adding up significantly, moving us toward $8 million.

Dale took to the phones to advance the Myers Park Presbyterian church-challenge grant announced at our press conference. Having been a minister in Charlotte for decades, he had an extensive network to call upon. Dale reached out to pastors from every house of faith to let their congregations know we needed them. He was persuasive. Methodist, Baptist, Catholic, Unitarian, and Jewish congregations joined the Presbyterians at every level. Some collected specific offerings for Moore Place, and we received the day's collection. Odd amounts, like $1,516 from St. Ann's Catholic or $2,351 from Avondale Presbyterian. Others gave thousands of dollars from their own capital campaigns, including $30,000 from mine, Christ Church, and $75,000 from Myers Park United Methodist in honor of a church member who had once been homeless.

With churches, foundations, and families donating, we had so much momentum that I asked a friend, Jan Shealy, to help me track it all. By November 23, 2009, only a month after our press conference, we had received checks and pledges totaling $8,116,000. Only $1,884,000 to go.

———

"Mom, get off the phone!" Maddie told me.

We were driving to the mountains for the holiday weekend, and I checked my cell at every stoplight. A reporter from the *Observer* was going to call me for a Thanksgiving article he was writing on Moore Place. The lead angle was that we had raised nearly a million dollars in the month since our press conference.

While I was glad for the publicity, I was nervous about the impact. A million dollars in one month was a huge story, but I didn't want people to think we didn't need their gifts. We still had a long way to go—almost $2 million. It was going to take another break-through gift like the Knight Foundation's to make this happen.

My cell phone rang in the car, and Emma grabbed it away. "Mom, it's Thanksgiving!"

"I know, but this could be important! What's the number?" She read it aloud, and I didn't recognize it.

"Okay, let it go to voice mail," I relented.

We turned up the radio, and I focused on singing, driving, and family. The twins were right. It was Thanksgiving, and I could for-get about Moore Place for a few days. Lauren and Kailey were both home from college, and it was the first time we had all been together since the summer.

When we arrived at the mountain house, we got busy with all the cooking. Having four daughters was the best for holidays because everyone had learned our family recipes and each had her own specialty. Lauren hand cut bread cubes for the sausage stuffing, Maddie kneaded and rolled the dough for the ham biscuits, Kailey created apple pies, and Emma made the cranberry sauce. Charlie was in charge of the turkey, so each year I focused on chopping onions and celery, mashing potatoes, and preparing green beans with almonds like Gigi used to make.

We spent the afternoon listening to music and bumping elbows in the kitchen until dinner. Every Thanksgiving, we always went around the table to say what we were grateful for.

"I am grateful Mom stayed off her phone and computer all afternoon," Maddie said.

We all laughed, but it made me remember that voice mail in the car I hadn't listened to. It was three hours later when the dishes were done before I finally played it.

"Kathy, this is Tom Lawrence with the Leon Levine Foundation."

Hugh McColl III and I had made a presentation to the Levine Foundation months before and submitted an application, but we hadn't heard back. They were the most prominent local foundation, and after months with no word, we assumed we had not made their priority list for the year.

"The Leon Levine Foundation is pleased to award a grant of $500,000 to Moore Place."

I knew what I was grateful for that Thanksgiving. I saved that voice mail on my phone for three years and played it over and over. That remarkable message would boost our year-end receipts to just over $9 million: an impossible amount, especially considering the Wells Fargo gift had been awarded only six months earlier.

———

With under a million dollars to go, I started getting nervous about delivering on what we had promised donors. Moore Place was going to be a home for people like Chilly Willy, Bill Halsey, and, hopefully, women like Christine—men and women who had been on the streets for decades. Their lives were complicated, and keeping them housed was going to be a daily challenge.

Moore Place was going to be only as good as the people running it. We needed to start with an incredibly effective executive director. I knew that job was over my head. During the last two years, I had been saved repeatedly by people such as Jerry Licari and the other Five Guys, who covered for my weaknesses. Now we needed someone who was qualified for this twenty-four-hours-a-day job.

Dale knew we needed someone as well. "We better start advertising now because it could take a long time to find someone."

I honestly had no idea who would take this job. The ad would need to read: "Must be fearless and have no personal life."

I didn't put that in the job description, but it was true. I knew what Joann gave up on a daily basis to keep the residents at Homeless to Homes going. The executive director was going to have her job times seven. I listed the position on a national nonprofit website and hoped somebody like Mother Teresa would apply.

———

There were 115 volunteers all over downtown Charlotte wearing purple T-shirts that read "Counting on Change." Liz Clasen-Kelly and I had been working for months on this event, the most important phase of Moore Place other than raising the money—finding out who in Charlotte needed Moore Place the most.

Common Ground had developed a survey of questions, the Vulnerability Index (VI), designed to determine which chronically homeless were most likely to die on the streets. With this knowledge we could systematically rather than subjectively prioritize the hundreds of men and women for the eighty-five apartments we would build.

We set the VI study for February 22–26, 2010, aiming to interview every chronically homeless person in Charlotte and create a priority list for Moore Place based on those most likely to die on the streets.

The system survey was straightforward; the implementation was daunting. Because Liz loved data, she led the project, organizing dozens of volunteers to help canvass the city from 5:00 a.m. until 10:00 p.m. every day for four days.

Common Ground sent three people from its staff to help us conduct this city-wide search for every chronically homeless person in Charlotte. Becky Kanis, the lead on our project, was like a general commanding the troops through the arduous survey process.

As we gathered stories and data, we realized the final conclusions were going to reveal a tally larger than we had imagined—807 people had been homeless more than a year, almost double our highest estimate. The data collected was going to be powerful in convincing the community that Charlotte did indeed have a long-ignored problem of chronic homelessness, and Moore Place was the solution.

At the end of the week, Becky and one of her coworkers from Common Ground arranged to meet me for dinner to celebrate our success. I had spent so much time with logistics and Becky that I had barely spoken to Caroline Chambre, who had also flown down to help.

When we finished ordering, Becky left the table to make a call. Caroline leaned over the table and quietly said, "I saw your ad."

"The ad for Moore Place executive director?"

She nodded.

I couldn't imagine why she was even looking.

"I grew up in Charlotte," Caroline said simply. "My dad's been sick and I've wanted to move back to help my mom for a long time, but I didn't think I could find a job like the one I have at Common Ground."

Caroline's résumé was better than I could have hoped for. She had even been the director of a property with 650 residents—Moore Place with eighty-five would be simple by comparison.

But there was one fact from her résumé I could not believe. Caroline had been on staff at the Prince George property—the very same one I had visited at Christmas two years before.

We hired her the next day.

Two months later she arrived from New York, and one of her first assignments was to go back to her own high school, South Mecklenburg, with Eugene Coleman. Their service club hosted an annual weeklong social justice fundraising campaign, and this year the students had picked Moore Place.

Coleman and Caroline were headed to the event when she asked if he had his speech ready.

"I know what I want to say," he said.

In a packed gymnasium full of fidgeting teenagers, Coleman came to the lectern and quietly gazed at the audience. He continued to stare, not moving, not saying a word.

Finally, after an uncomfortable silence, Coleman leaned into the microphone and spoke softly. "Can you see me?"

Caroline, and maybe the gathered students, thought he was asking if they had a good view of the stage. Some students shifted in their seats.

Another long pause.

"Can you see me?" Coleman asked again.

This time the question was more disturbing.

"That's important," Coleman said. "Because for twenty years, I didn't think anyone saw me. Nobody could see me because I didn't want to be seen. Drugs took all my pride, robbed me of every piece of self-respect, every dream I ever had. But somehow God saw fit to give me a second chance. And that second chance is people like you."

Coleman went on to share much of his personal story. Afterward students and staff stood in line to tell him about their connections: a father who was homeless, a brother on the streets, time spent with family in a shelter. Even the school security guard confessed that her own brother was a meth addict, homeless in Charleston, South Carolina. She added her own $60 to the total of more than $6,000 collected by students to help make Moore Place more than a dream.

twenty-two

JUST LISTEN

Never be so focused on what you are looking for
that you overlook the thing you actually find.

—Ann Patchett[1]

Gifts like those from the high school service club, along with additional donations throughout spring 2010, inched us toward $9,500,000. We hoped the final $500,000 would come from the City of Charlotte.

In the past two years so many had worked together on this effort to solve the city's homeless problem—churches, foundations, corporations, even children running lemonade stands. We had also finally received support from the state of North Carolina for $500,000, and the county had created an ongoing partnership by paying the salaries of five social workers for Moore Place.

Everyone but the City of Charlotte had chipped in. On June 14, 2010, Dale, Liz, Caroline, and I sat in the auditorium where the council held their meetings. We nervously waited through the nineteen agenda items on the docket before ours. Before starting Moore Place, I was not aware of who was on the city council or even that they held these meetings. Staring at the panel in front of me, I now knew the name of every councilperson and how they were likely to vote. The meeting started at 7:00 p.m. At 8:59 p.m. the vote for $500,000 for Moore Place was called. We collectively held our breath.

Nine in favor. One opposed—the representative from our neighborhood where the junkyard waited to be transformed. We passed. It was our final yes.

Crossing this last fundraising hurdle was exhilarating. After all the months, all the work, all the dreaming, we actually were going to do this. At the office I was feeling heroic, but at home my intense focus on this project came with a high cost.

I had been so consumed with doing good I had forgotten to love well.

The day I realized this I was working from home, trying to distract myself with e-mails. In truth I was focused on Kailey, who was upstairs, hidden behind her bedroom door. Kailey was home for the summer after her freshman year of college at a prestigious California school. The spring semester had been particularly rough, and she had made the decision to transfer to an East Coast university. Charlie and I couldn't decide if her decision had been prompted by the long distance from family and friends or something else.

I contemplated her closed door. Should I knock?

No, I was sure she was fine. I would give her some more time. I tried to return to Moore Place and my in-box. Staring at my computer screen, I attempted to concentrate on the day's work. There were several e-mails from the Charlotte Housing Authority I could start with. Even though we had all the money raised, we still couldn't begin construction. Since we were taking some government money, we had to wait for federal approval to move forward. Four months had passed with no word from the government. We couldn't get the regional employee to push through the application, so I was constantly fielding questions from donors to explain why we had not started construction.

As worried as I was about all that, I was more concerned about the problem upstairs. Kailey had been in her room for hours, so I went to check on her again. Slowly I climbed the stairs, but her door was still closed. I could see no light from under the door.

Pausing halfway up the flight of stairs, I sat down and tried to calm the sense of dread that had been choking me all morning. The dread really had started the day before with a letter I found in the trash can. It had been Kailey's twentieth birthday, and in typical fashion, she had torn through her presents. Discarded wrapping paper, boxes, and ribbon had left a foot-high heap on the table. Charlie, always the cleaner, had scooped up behind her, not checking to see whether all the boxes were empty or full. In the process a beautiful pair of earrings had gone missing, and I was sure they were in the trash.

Searching the outdoor trash can, some thickly folded pages caught my eye. Four papers torn from a legal pad had been haphazardly shoved into the bag of giftwrap in an attempt to make them disappear forever. But it was Kailey's handwriting that I couldn't stop staring at.

I took the journal pages from the trash and sat down to read them. The words took my breath away. My daughter was desperately depressed. The girl who had written these words, I did not know. The girl who had written these words needed help.

I don't know how long I stayed in the backyard trying to absorb it. How could I have missed how unhappy she was? I had vowed to be like Gigi and curl up on the couch with my daughters and always listen.

From the time Lauren and Kailey and the twins were little, I always tried to be there when they got home from school. I loved being the mom who knew the lyrics to their songs and volunteered to drive the late shift from the school dances so I could be in on the gossip.

How could it be that Kailey had become so lost without my knowing? How could it be that I had spent the past two years getting to know people like Coleman, Raymond, and Chilly Willy, yet I didn't even know my own daughter?

The pages stayed in my pocket all day, waiting for Charlie to get home so we could talk with Kailey together. It was hard to function with the burning shame; I felt like a failure as a mom. I had heard the saying, "You are only as happy as your saddest child." Now I understood.

When we had sat down with the letter, Kailey looked first at the papers and then at each of us. She held Charlie's gaze a little longer. They had always had some sort of unspoken communication, like whale sonar. I swear they could speak sentences without a sound. A paragraph of pain passed between them. A tear began to roll down her cheek, and she stared at her hands.

"I didn't want to worry you," Kailey said softly. "I didn't know what to say."

We agreed she needed to see a doctor, and I thought of Jane Harrell. She had helped Scott Mercer even before he knew anything was wrong. She had surprisingly put a check for Moore Place in my pocket. Somehow I sensed the reason we had come to know each other was so she could help Kailey. I sent her a text, and she called right away even though it was 9:30 at night.

"She will be fine, Kathy, I'm telling you. So many college kids struggle, and no one talks about it," Jane assured me. "You send her to my office tomorrow, and we'll make a plan."

Now I paced outside Kailey's door, waiting desperately for her to wake up so we could make that plan. I did better with plans, with lists and ways to fix things. As I stared at her door, wondering what she was feeling and thinking on the other side, I thought about my mom's bedroom door. How many times coming home from school had I looked at that closed door? How many times had I waited for that door to open?

I couldn't remember ever wondering what my mom was feeling on the other side. As long as I stayed on one side, I didn't have to feel. I didn't have to know. But this was my daughter. Her pain. Her problems. Her door couldn't keep me from feeling. No door, no distance, could keep me from sharing her pain.

There was a bump and a shuffling as Kailey moved from her bedroom to the bathroom. I waited before gently opening her door.

"Kailey?"

She was sitting in bed in her gray school sweatshirt that had paint splotches on it from when she had gone to help rebuild homes in New Orleans after Hurricane Katrina. Ripped, torn, and stained, it was still her favorite. She hugged her knees and looked up at me expectantly.

What could I say? It will get better? Everything will be okay?

I didn't know how to make her feel better. Moms are supposed to be able to make their kids feel better. Normally I had a long list of suggestions for my girls. I was the ultimate fixer. You should do this. You should try that. Let's make a list. Let's make a plan. I always had lots of advice, lots of words. I could talk and find a solution for any problem. Over the years I thought this was what I wanted my girls to see and learn from me. I wanted to be a strong, capable example for them. Like my dad had taught me, I wanted them to know they could do anything, be anything. I never cried or let them see me quitting. If there was a problem, I didn't feel it, I just fixed it.

But for this, I had no fix. No solution. No words.

I climbed next to her in bed and pulled her head onto my shoulder. We both began to cry. Me, slow, sad tears. Kailey, heaving sobs. We didn't speak. We just cried until we couldn't anymore. Finally she spoke.

"You know, Mom, this is all I ever wanted. I didn't want you to fix anything," she confessed. "I just wanted you to hold me and listen."

With construction on hold and Caroline Chambre in charge, I spent the rest of that summer focusing on family. Ever since the pack trip in Wyoming with Lauren and Kailey, our family had started taking more adventurous vacations. We tried to pick remote and rugged ranches with little cell phone or Internet access. That way neither of us, especially Charlie, could be pulled into work. That year we planned a Colorado dude ranch vacation for hiking, horseback riding, and fishing. The week was so relaxing. No decisions to be made. No meetings to attend. No donors to update.

Toward the end of our stay, Charlie was distracted by a lengthy conference call. With no cell service, he had to use the phone in our log cabin, so he was stuck in a chair next to the wood wall for over an hour while we waited for him to go on our last family horseback ride of the vacation.

"Charlie," I whispered. "Let's go."

He gave me the one-minute sign. I sighed. Sometimes I hated his job. Whatever it was, however, apparently needed his undivided attention. I heard him hang up and call quietly to me.

"Kathy, can we talk a minute?" He looked serious. "So there's a problem in the New York office," he began. "And they want me to work on it."

"Okay . . ." I wasn't getting it. Charlie rarely talked about work. The girls joked that he worked for the CIA because he never talked about what he did.

"So they are asking that I go to New York to work on it." He paused and looked at me. "As in move."

"Move? To New York? When?"

He nodded. "Like next month. I know there's a lot to consider," Charlie said. "We can talk about it."

We both knew we could talk about it, but we both knew what would happen. Charlie was going to New York. When work asked, it wasn't really a question.

We said nothing to the girls and headed out for our ride. I tried to forget about it the best I could, but my brain doesn't work that way. My brain generates ideas and options.

Throughout the trail ride I considered possibilities. We could get an apartment. We could commute. We wouldn't sell our house. Nothing would change. I could do it all.

We were in a huge pasture, looking back at the ranch. The girls were begging the wrangler for one more family race. The horses took off with just the slightest nudge. I think the animals loved running wild as much as we did. Nose-to-tail saddle rides must be as boring for horses as they were for guests. Charlie was in the lead with Lauren and Kailey right on his horse's flank. Emma was in the middle with Maddie and me bringing up the rear. I gave my horse a kick with my boot to urge him ahead of Maddie's horse. We were loping side by side less than two feet apart. Maddie was laughing her full-out belly laugh. Her horse turned his head slightly to see us gaining on him and midstride thrust out his powerful back right leg, landing the kick somewhere between my horse's stomach and hindquarters.

My horse pitched forward and then abruptly stopped galloping.

I lurched over the saddle horn, trying to hold on. Successfully staying in the saddle, I thought I had saved the disastrous fall. Then my horse unexpectedly reared. Screaming as I fell off, I collided with the ground. There was a roar in my ears as I stared at the sky, trying to make sense of how I got there. I remember staring at the clouds thinking, *That was out of control.*

By now the wrangler, Charlie, and the girls had all ridden back to help me. Charlie was leaning over me asking if I was hurt. I couldn't answer because I wasn't sure.

My head hurt, my back hurt, my hand hurt. Were they broken? Why were ants crawling on me? Charlie and the wrangler moved me gently as they assessed for broken bones. In a field full of rocks, I apparently had landed on a red anthill. A soft red anthill. A ten-inch mound of dirt that, even though filled with angry ants, had saved my spine.

After a trip to the emergency room by pickup truck, I came back to the ranch that night with a chipped bone in my right hand and a collar to support my sprained neck. It wasn't the injuries that kept me up that night, but the thought I had as I lay on the ground.

That was out of control.

It felt like I had just received a giant sign from the universe: slow down.

Live in New York and Charlotte? And lead Moore Place? And be a good mom to four daughters, one of whom had already tried to tell me to sit still and listen a little more?

I was on my back again, this time staring up at the ceiling as Charlie snored. We had to get up at 5:00 a.m. to catch the plane back to Charlotte, but I couldn't sleep.

Three years had passed since Denver asked me, "Where are the beds?" Three years of waking up every day and trying to figure out how to house homeless people. Three years, and I had let everything else come second to that one Moore Place goal. We were almost there.

Didn't I want to still be in charge? Didn't I need to still be in charge?

I knew in my heart the answer. This past year had been incredibly difficult, but I had stayed because of my commitment to Dale Mullennix and my new family of Coleman, Raymond, and others. I had learned that about myself—I didn't quit on people. But now it was time to put my people first. Charlie. Lauren. Kailey. Emma. Maddie. They had taken a back seat for the past three years. Denver, Dale, and Moore Place had all come first. I had lived the Do Good. It was time to live a little more of the Love Well.

I kept hearing a whisper, and this time I didn't think I was crazy. *Tell Dale it's time.*

twenty-three

THE LAST, BEST YES

The most beautiful people we have known are those who have known defeat, known suffering, known struggle, known loss, and have found their way out of those depths. These persons have an appreciation, a sensitivity, and an understanding of life that fills them with compassion, gentleness, and a deep loving concern. Beautiful people do not just happen.

—Elisabeth Kübler-Ross[1]

My cell phone vibrated on my lap in the back seat of the taxi, and I looked down at the number I easily recognized: Caroline. We talked a lot by cell phone these days. I had told Dale it was time I stopped being a part-time employee, but I couldn't really quit, so I went back to full-time volunteer status. It had been six months since Charlie and I had begun our new commuting lifestyle. He went to New York on Mondays and usually came back on Thursdays to spend the weekend in Charlotte. I joined him in Manhattan when I could.

We were almost empty nesters with Maddie and Emma juniors in high school, Lauren a senior in college, and Kailey now a sophomore back on the East Coast. Since opening up to us and Jane about what was happening, Kailey was learning how to manage anxiety and depression. The office in the train depot was now all Caroline's, and she had become the executive director of Moore Place even though we still technically didn't have a Moore Place. For more than eleven months we had been ready to start construction but couldn't break ground without approval from the US Department of Housing and Urban Development.

While we waited on the government, Caroline had tried to be creative, working on everything from selecting paint colors to collecting résumés for future employees. I realized I had never thought about these details. Honestly, the actual construction process was overwhelming to me.

Where would the trash chute go? Were there enough fire exits? Did the handicap-access rooms have wide-enough doorways?

Caroline easily answered all the questions and made suggestions based on the New York buildings she had managed.

When I gave up my job, I thought I would miss all the day-to-day details of the work, but it was the people I missed most. The program lunches with Raymond ordering two pieces of pie to go. The e-mails from Dale, excited about a new donor or progress on the capital campaign. In New York I could go all day without talking to anyone until Charlie came back to the apartment for dinner.

The phone buzzed again on my lap. "Are you sitting down?" Caroline asked.

"Yes, actually in a yellow cab," I said. The roar of traffic made it difficult to hear, so I pressed my hand over my other ear. "What's up?"

"It finally came!" she said. "Our approval from HUD! We finally got it!"

I screamed out loud in the taxi, and the driver turned his head, alarmed.

"Sorry!" I said pointing to the phone. "Can you believe it? Eleven months! Eleven months it took them!"

The last, best yes.

"I've checked calendars with the mayor and all the major donors, and the best date for the grand opening is Sunday, January 29, 2012," Caroline said.

I smiled at the huge God-instance. Should I tell her?

"Kathy? Is that okay with you?" Caroline asked.

"It works great for me," I admitted. "January 29 is my forty-ninth birthday."

When I called Ron Hall to let him know the date, I found out news about Denver that was not so good.

"We would love to come," Ron said. "But I don't think there is any way Denver can make the trip. He's having trouble with blood clots in his legs, and winter travel is especially hard. Maybe we can send a video for you to play of our congratulations."

When I had asked Denver about naming the building after him, he said, "You better hurry because I'm old." He might not be there to see it, but my promise would be kept, and Denver's name would be on the doors—forever.

"Kathy, it's so nice!" Mom said as we drove into the parking lot of Moore Place. "I didn't expect it to look so nice!"

I smiled because I knew what she meant. The light yellow siding. The bright white trim. The red roof. The newly planted bushes. It didn't look like a shelter for homeless people. It looked like a home. It was the day before the grand opening, and I was taking my mom on a private tour. She had flown in for the big event along with my sister Allyson.

Louise would miss the grand opening for a long-planned sabbatical in Costa Rica, but her faith had gotten me here. It had been four years since I confessed to her and Charlie that Denver called me to "build beds" and she directed me to Common Ground.

As my mom, Allyson, and I entered Moore Place through the glass doors, it felt perfectly full circle that Mom would be the first to officially tour. If my mom had not mentioned *Same Kind of Different As Me* to me, I doubt I ever would have read it.

In front of us was the donor wall—everyone who had even given $5 on the display. Across the top in gray script it read: "To those who brought us home: Thank you."

Listed underneath were the hundreds of people who had made this residence possible, most of whom I didn't know five years ago. Now every name meant something.

- 168 individuals whose combined donations totaled $990,101
- 28 foundations who together contributed $6,423,000
- 60 houses of faith with a total contribution of $479,512
- state, local, and federal funds totaling $2,700,000

Although Steve Barton and David Furman had created an incredible building, the number of people who had made it financially possible was truly amazing. Eight teenagers had a bake sale to raise $550. Two Davidson College students cycled across the United States, raising over $8,000. And the Mailbox Angel continued to send her $5 and $10 gifts steadily and faithfully. Each name was a story. Each had given all they had in order to make this happen.

As I walked the halls with my mother and sister, volunteers moved around us, getting ready for the celebration the next day.

Homeless to Homes residents were going to be giving tours after the ceremony. Model apartments were being readied as volunteers made beds, hung shower curtains, and stocked kitchens. Every item in the eighty-five apartments had been donated by a family, book club, or church group in our Home for the Holidays donation drive.

I gave Mom and Allyson the full tour of the apartments, each flooded with sunshine from large windows in every home. The library shelves were being filled with donated books for the residents to borrow.

As we toured the art center, Mom wore a contemplative expression as she surveyed the easels and art supplies. I thought she was remembering the art studio in our home, but she surprised us by saying, "You know, I wanted to be an art therapist."

Allyson and I looked at each other. "What? You did?"

"Yes!" she said, looking up. "You didn't know? That's why I went back to school to get my master's after you girls went to college. I wanted to bring some kind of joy to those psych wards."

"Wait, what happened?" Allyson asked.

"Well, your dad got diagnosed with cancer and that was the end of that," she said, looking back into the art center wistfully.

We rarely talked about it. Those Lost Years. We still acted like none of it ever happened. Mom seemed to think it was better that way.

"What good does it do to rehash the past?" she would say.

But there in the halls of Moore Place, filled with hope for so many, it seemed the right time to examine some of those wounds that had never truly healed.

"I always wanted to be there for you girls, but then it would happen again," Mom said with a huge emphasis on *again*. Her shoulders slumped, and she looked defeated, as if she could sense an imminent hospital stay.

There it was: the shame, the secret, and the thing we could never talk about.

Mom's version of "again" was so different than how it all could have been. Any one of those agains could have been the end. Each spiral into mania could have been a suicide. With each round of new medicine, she could have stopped taking them. The pain of each lost year could have been amplified if she had coped using alcohol. None of that was her story. None of that became my story.

Mom always got up. She always fought her way back. Hers was the ultimate story of survival. Seven times down, eight times up. Yet she still didn't understand the power of her own story. Truthfully I never had either.

I had spent nearly my whole life carrying a quiet grudge. I had never been able to truly forgive my mom. For going away. For leaving my idyllic childhood. For getting lost in the desert. But especially for not talking about it. For pretending it never happened. If we could talk about it, maybe I could finally let it go.

I looked at my mom and saw her as if for the first time in over forty years. The mom whose brain was brilliant and broken. My truth was not that I didn't have a mother growing up. My truth was I had lost her. I had lost that mom who was poised to give me the perfect childhood and then couldn't. I still missed that mom every day.

But who knows how that little girl with the perfect mother would have grown up? Who knows what she would have done with her life? That little girl never would have learned how strong she could be. That little girl never would have had to become resilient. That little girl never would have believed she could *do anything—really anything.*

I tried to tell her the truth. "All those years I was never thinking, *Some day this is going to make me incredibly resilient.*"

Mom smiled.

"But it did, and I am. And without all that I would not have moved to Charlotte or met Charlie or had my four girls or ever attempted to help a single homeless person. Your story is my story, Mom, and your story gave me all that."

We stood together in the moment, and the past forty years, including those sixteen Lost Years, were with us. Seconds earlier those years had been wedged between us, but it felt like they had just begun to compress in a time warp pulling together in an accordion of forgiveness.

We did not speak; we just felt. For the first time I could remember, we all just felt together. Not in secret. Not in shame. Not isolated in silence behind closed doors. Together. Taking in a sadness. Feeling a regret. Not fixing, just feeling.

That day I took a photo of my mom standing in front of Moore Place on the lot that had once been a junkyard. The sun was shining, and the sky was incredibly blue for a January day. She was smiling broadly in the foreground, Moore Place a backdrop to her happiness.

———

At the grand opening the next day, I was in the lobby greeting more than two hundred friends and donors as they arrived to fill the Moore Place dining room. Even though it wasn't my personal birthday party, it felt like one. Charlie and the girls arrived with his parents, Bob and Jean Izard, from New York. Before we had a single private donor to Moore Place, Bob and Jean had gone in with Charlie to be the very first donors to the capital campaign. They mailed their surprise pledge to Dale Mullennix and asked that the lobby be named in my honor. Showing them the plaque, I felt like I had received the best birthday present ever.

Dale began the program, recognizing John and Pat Moore with

a piece of original art by an artist in the UMC Artworks program. Then Dale called me forward and gave me another piece of art. It was a fifteen-by-fifteen-inch oil painting of a set of keys painted by a formerly homeless artist who would be moving into his own apartment later that week. I remember accepting the piece and turning around to see the audience standing and clapping.

Everyone there, from the Five Guys to Joann to Coleman to Liz, was part of this story. All these people whom I hadn't known four years ago played a role in this journey. Even before we all met, they already knew they were coming, Denver had assured me. Every person had a story, and now those hundreds of stories had built this home.

I should have thanked each one of them and said every name aloud, but I couldn't speak. There was too much to say, and no words matched what I was feeling. Charlie was standing, clapping with the crowd, tears in his eyes. This had been a long road for both of us. He had been the First Believer when I told him I wanted to start this crazy project. As obsessed and distracted as I had become, he never asked me to quit. I stepped off the stage and gave Charlie a long hug and then sat down with my family—all of them.

As I pulled myself together, Caroline spoke. She was poised and confident, describing how residents would move from a life of chaos to a life of normalcy. The new staff at Moore Place would help "create the ordinary." How extraordinary that would be for eighty-five men and women.

As Caroline spoke, I felt my incessant need to get this done fall away. It was finally finished. I had completed my promise to Denver and imagined the unimaginable for my father. Together, with all those in the room, we had done something about it. I would be stepping away after the grand opening. Caroline would run Moore Place, and I had worked my way out of a job. It felt like a natural transition, one for which I was grateful.

I might have been the birth mother to Moore Place, but Caroline would raise the child. Our baby couldn't be in better hands.

After the ceremony there were hugs, high fives, and home tours. In one final full-circle moment, the last person to ask me for a tour that day was Rufus Dalton, the same man who had been honored four years ago for his forty-year service to Outward Bound. That was the dinner after which Charlie and I wondered what would be our "forty-year thing."

When I saw him in the lobby waiting, I was stunned.

Was this God showing off again?

I wanted to tell Mr. Dalton that this whole project started years ago with his recognition dinner and the discussion Charlie and I had on the way home. I tried to find the words to tell Rufus how unreal it was to see him standing there in the Moore Place lobby on Opening Day. But I had no idea how to make him understand all that had happened since that night.

twenty-four

I FEEL LIKE PEOPLE NOW

And once the storm is over, you won't remember how
you made it through, how you managed to survive. You
won't even be sure, in fact, whether the storm is really
over. But one thing is certain. When you come out of the
storm you won't be the same person who walked in.
That's what the storm is all about.

—Haruki Murakami[1]

After almost five years of wishing and waiting, one of the first tenants to move in was Chilly Willy.

It took Dale, Liz, Caroline, and Chilly Willy's brother, Johnny, to convince Charlotte's most famous street person that this wasn't a trick. Moore Place wasn't a jail or a lock-down facility but truly a home of his own. It happened that his move-in date would be Valentine's Day 2012.

That morning Caroline was on high alert as she waited to

welcome Chilly Willy home, finally fulfilling the promise that Moore Place could successfully house Charlotte's own Million-Dollar Larry. As the day wore on, no one saw him. Caroline called Johnny to see if he knew where Chilly Willy was, but it seemed he had gone missing.

Had Chilly Willy really forgotten about the big day? Or had he just decided he couldn't come inside to live?

Finally, late in the afternoon, Caroline spotted Chilly Willy in the parking lot. She went outside to meet him and was surprised to find him completely sober.

He announced he had checked himself into the city "drunk tank" to clean up for his momentous day. And one more thing—he was no longer Chilly Willy. He told Caroline that from this day forward, he was giving up his street name, and he wanted everyone to call him by his birth name: William Larry Major.

A couple of weeks later Liz Clasen-Kelly handed me a note from Larry. To this day I carry his letter with me, along with a group photo of the first thirteen Homeless to Homes residents. Both are tucked in the front pocket of my black meeting notebook.

> Ms. Kathy Izard
> I'm William Larry Major. Will you come visit me?
> I'm doing good and I feel much better. I love my place, I feel like people now.
> > Thanks you'er [sic] friend,
> > William L. Major

Also among the new residents was soup kitchen cowboy Bill Halsey and his brown leather hat. Bill was that kind cowboy who had stood up for me in the soup kitchen and lived in his hole in the ground for years. We were thrilled to be able to give Bill a home finally, but it turned out that wasn't the best part of his move into Moore Place.

For years Bill's mother had been praying about him. She did not know how to help her homeless son or even where to find him, but she knew he got meals and mail at the UMC. Along with praying, she wrote to him at the center's address.

When Bill found out he was going to be housed at Moore Place, he proudly called his mom to let her know. Mrs. Halsey was there for her son's move-in day with tears in her eyes.

"I always prayed this day would come," she confessed to Caroline. "I followed the stories about Moore Place in the newspaper and hoped one day my son would find his way here."

What dear Mrs. Halsey didn't admit was that she had done more than pray and send letters to her son.

Even after Moore Place was built, the pastel envelopes from our Mailbox Angel kept coming with notes of encouragement and the words *May God Bless and Multiply this small amount*. Now they were addressed to the Moore Place mailbox instead of the UMC, yet there we still had no way to thank the giver personally. Caroline would record the contributions as I had under Anonymous, wondering who our long-time benefactor might be.

Then one day, after receiving another Angel envelope, Caroline noticed something different—maybe a mistake. This time in the top left-hand corner of the pastel envelope there was a name: Lily Halsey.

Caroline couldn't wait to call. "Kathy, you are not going to believe this. Our Mailbox Angel is Bill Halsey's mom!"

———

I had not talked to Ron Hall since I sent him the photos from the grand opening, so I was surprised to see his number on my cell phone two months later, April 1, 2012.

"Hey, Ron!" I said.

"Kathy, Denver died last night in his sleep."

I couldn't even process what Ron said. Everything I knew about Denver had been so otherworldly; I think I assumed he was immortal.

The last time I had seen Denver was March 6, 2008. Four months after that first True Blessings, our founding team—Sarah, Kim, Angela, and I—decided to take a trip to Texas to visit Ron and Denver. At the time I was just starting my new job at the UMC, and I wanted to see what kind of beds they had in Denver's hometown. We were excited to spend time with Ron and Denver again and tour the Fort Union Gospel Mission they had written about in their book. We arranged a dinner with the two of them, but when we arrived at the restaurant, only Ron was waiting. Denver, as customary, was nowhere to be found.

"He'll be along," Ron promised.

Ron filled the dinner hour with stories of the past year and all the places they had spoken.

"We've been approached for a movie deal!" he told us. "Denver wants Forest Whitaker to play him!"

Dinner progressed, entrees arrived and were cleared, but Denver hadn't come. Angela's right leg shook nervously as she checked her watch and stared at the restaurant entrance, willing Denver to arrive.

"Ron, we really wanted to see Denver again and hear all his wisdom!" Sarah confided.

Ron tried Denver's cell phone several times but got no answer.

The evening was coming to a close, and we thought Denver was going to stand us up. When Denver finally made his grand entrance, he looked like a movie star dressed in a flashy new suit with pinstripes. He wore sunglasses even though it was 10:00 p.m. Restaurant guests obviously recognized the homeless man turned celebrity author, and many wanted to speak with him. Denver nodded at people and accepted handshakes from the most insistent fans.

Finally reaching our table, he shook his head, telling us, "I don't understand why they all want to shake my hand now. None of them wanted to touch me when I was homeless."

Denver held court with us for the next hour, telling stories and throwing out Denverisms:

> Our limitation is God's opportunity. When you get all the way to the end of your rope and there ain't nothin' you can do, that's when God takes over.

Sarah brought out a small notebook and pen and tried to transcribe the circuitous philosophical mind of Denver Moore. Later we all flipped through the pages and agreed there was no way to do his musings justice. There was something about Denver that couldn't be captured on paper. Being in his presence was undeniably remarkable. His words gave you goose bumps only when they were delivered with those dark eyes drilling into your soul.

I wondered what Denver saw with those eyes. Did he see like the rest of us, or could he see something different? Had Denver ever really even seen me, or, like Coleman, was I invisible? Was Denver ever really giving me, Kathy Izard, a message? Or, since "white folk look alike," was he just speaking about the injustices of homelessness while I happened to be standing there, feeling responsible for something?

I may have had a four-year obsession to fulfill my promise to him, but I am convinced Denver Moore never knew my name—first or last. All the same, I would never forget him. Meeting Denver had triggered my spiritual awakening. It marked the beginning of my efforts to make everything previously invisible, indelibly visible. I had promised Denver I would build beds and promised myself I would finish before he died.

We had just made it.

—

The grand opening just before Denver's death and Larry's Valentine's Day move-in would have been a Hollywood happy ending for this story. But real life is much messier.

Six months after Denver died, on October 19, 2012, I woke to an early morning text from Caroline sent late the night before: Larry is dead. Car accident on 7th Street. Will be convening staff early in a.m. Am in shock. Just leaving building.

I was in shock too. In the past twenty years, Larry, aka Chilly Willy, had survived prison, muggings, illness, heat waves, and ice storms. I remembered Johnny telling me about the regular phone calls from friends asking if Chilly Willy was dead because they hadn't seen him on the streets in a while. Always the rumors were untrue—not this time.

I called Caroline immediately.

"I thought it was a mistake again, Kathy. You know how everyone always would say he had died, but we'd find out he was in jail or something?" Caroline was having trouble talking. "But, this time, it's true," she finished.

William Larry Major, fifty-eight, was dead. A car outside a neighborhood bar had struck him. The driver was a sixty-five-year-old woman, undoubtedly traumatized but not charged.

Caroline sounded exhausted and shaky. Not only had she been fielding phone calls all night from distraught residents of Moore Place, she was blaming herself about how it could have played out differently.

"I've been trying to think what I could have done," she said.

The truth was Caroline had, beyond all probability, kept Larry housed and very much alive for eight months. Many times after moving in, Larry had given his Moore Place apartment key to Caroline, saying he couldn't do it anymore. Each time, she had given it back, assuring him he could.

I hung up with Caroline and searched the Internet, where it seems information about almost anything can be found. Larry's death was no exception. I immediately located a *Charlotte Observer* news article, a blog post by a local writer, an RIP Chilly Willy Facebook page, and a YouTube video with a thousand hits and counting of Larry singing, all posted within hours of his death. I watched the video and smiled at Larry's gravelly voice belting out his favorite Charlie Daniel's Band song, "Long Haired Country Boy," one last time.

My cell interrupted the video, and I saw it was Liz. I answered my phone with, "I heard," and was surprised to find I could not speak without crying.

Liz was even more distraught. Her concern for Larry, whose addiction and pain played out publicly on Charlotte's streets, had helped write the moral and economic case for Moore Place. His story of cycling needlessly in and out of jails and hospitals had inspired John and Pat Moore to call Dale with their extraordinary first gift for the pilot program in 2008. That had changed the lives of dozens of chronically homeless in Charlotte, including Coleman, Raymond, and Ruth and, finally, Larry himself.

At the end of our call, Liz made a comment I carry with me still. "When I saw in the paper that they wrote 'formerly homeless,' I took comfort in that."

There was, as Liz said, mercy in Larry's story. He hadn't frozen under a bridge or been beaten to death. And while Larry was so proud to finally have his own place, he was still struggling with how to start a life for the first time in two decades.

In the days that followed, Charlotte overflowed with love for William Larry Major. Radio and TV stations ran stories, the *Charlotte Observer* wrote two feature articles, the online obituary guest book logged 294 entries, and that Facebook tribute page grew to more than ten thousand views. Larry, in his own wild way, had been a community talisman. People wrote of his humor, wisdom, and innate sweetness. They told of how he had offered a kind word, a song, or a joke. Apparently he was known in neighborhoods I didn't even know he wandered.

Larry's family held a service for him on October 22, 2012, in the church Larry's father had started. Several hundred people stood in line outside the church to pay their respects. It was the most diverse crowd I had ever been with in Charlotte. Every age, every income, and every race was represented among the mourners, all patiently waiting to come inside the overflowing church.

While waiting in line, I stood beside a police officer, sheriff, EMT worker, and city bus driver, each recalling how the free-spirited Larry impacted their lives. At the front of the church were photos of Larry during his days at Moore Place: winning at Bingo, flashing a peace sign to the camera at a picnic. Two handmade posters had been signed by dozens of Moore Place friends, one poster reading, "Ride your Harley to Heaven! In Loving Memory."

Larry's family asked that memorials be made to Moore Place, and after the service they scattered Larry's ashes on the streets of Charlotte—the place he loved the most.

twenty-five

GOD WAS IN IT

"WELL NOW YOU KNOW HOW I FEEL ABOUT
GOD," said Owen Meany. "I CAN'T SEE HIM—
BUT I ABSOLUTELY KNOW HE IS THERE!"

—John Irving[1]

Now I knew the ending to Denver's and Larry's stories, but I still couldn't write the next chapter of mine. With Moore Place open I wasn't really needed. I had no idea what to make of the last few years or what I should do for the next decade. If I was no longer Graphics Girl or Homeless to Homes director, who was I? What was I supposed to do with all this newfound knowledge about fundraising? If I had felt this one purpose so clearly, would there ever be another?

Allyson thought I could do some soul searching at her favorite retreat center, Kripalu, a former seminary turned yoga center in the Berkshires. She invited my mom and me to a workshop with English poet and philosopher David Whyte. I agreed to go even though I had never heard of him.

I had come prepared for the workshop with pen and paper, ready to absorb all David Whyte's wisdom, but I was disappointed when he offered no handouts, no slides, and no PowerPoint presentations. It seemed there were no life lessons starred and highlighted in his lectures. If I was looking for takeaways, I was going to have to really listen and find them myself.

My attention drifted as the poet enigmatically recited his poems at the front of the large room, chanting really. It took me a few minutes to realize he was quoting everything from memory. He did not pause for effect in the natural places or even finish the entire work. He rolled through lines, stopping and starting like a dance instructor repeating steps. Then these lines from his poem "The Journey" brought me to full attention:

> Sometimes everything
> has to be
> inscribed across
> the heavens
>
> so you can find
> the one line
> already written
> inside you.

That was amazing.

I felt like this poet had pulled up a chair to my psyche and given me the CliffsNotes to my life. That one sentence described all the God-instances and serendipity and grace that began with a book and ended with an apartment building. But really that one sentence explained how a lost six-year-old who missed her mother could end up a resilient forty-nine-year-old able to believe she could do anything.

David Whyte continued with his poem, but I could not hear him. I just stared at the sentence I had jotted down in my notes as he spoke. I paused at his words about what was written in me. How did they get there, those metaphorical words inside me? Did it happen when my parents named me Katherine Grace, or did it start sooner, back when they were two college sweethearts reading scriptures to each other?

And now these three remain: faith, hope and love. But the greatest of these is love.[2]

Their love had been bruised and broken and hospitalized and even parted by death, but Mom was still here. Still trying to learn at age eighty. Still listening to life. Still keeping over thirty years' worth of "All my love, Leighton" cards bound tightly with a rubber band. I looked over at her. Mom's hands were folded across her chest as she sat. She stared intently ahead, listening to the poet's words.

Mom smiled imperceptibly as the poet spoke about "the ashes of life." I knew she was thinking: the Phoenix. Her private symbol.

The Phoenix signifies the fabled purple bird that rises from the ashes after perishing in a fire of its own making.

Mom views her life, her story, similar to that of the Phoenix. She was able to withstand and survive all those fires of mania. My whole life I believed my foundations came mostly from my dad: do good, work hard, change the world. Throughout our lives, Dad had given each of his three daughters a compass to search for a bigger purpose. I had almost overlooked my mother's quieter messages, which I needed for this journey maybe even more: faith and resilience. In truth, by recommending *Same Kind of Different As Me*, my mother had given me the key to my greatest gift—my calling.

My mom. The Phoenix. Rising from the ashes.

My childhood. My life. Perfectly imperfect, so I could finally see the one line that was already written inside me.

———

As I looked back on the journey of Moore Place, it seemed all the dots had been connected except one: Mrs. Halsey. Caroline had met her but I never had. Thinking about all that had happened and all the God-instances, I needed to tell Lily Halsey that what she did had mattered—that a Hallmark card cradling a blessing and a few dollars had made all the difference to me.

Lily Halsey and her cards. My mom and her cards. My mom's habit had always quietly irritated me. I couldn't value it in my own mother until I could value it in someone else's mother. This care. This connection. This compassion. It wasn't a waste of time for Lily Halsey to send me all those cards. It had meant everything to me.

It wasn't silly for my mom to track the birthdays, anniversaries, and holidays and send literally hundreds of cards a year. Thousands in her lifetime. It was her ministry.

I drove to Huntersville, North Carolina, to finally meet Lily Halsey, my mysterious Mailbox Angel, who now lived in an assisted living facility. A nurse helped me find her. She was sitting in a wheelchair by the front door, talking with a friend, and I came up behind her.

"Mrs. Halsey?"

A woman with soft gray hair turned to gaze up at me, two sky-blue eyes searching my face for recognition.

She clearly didn't know me, but I would have known her anywhere. Those same blue eyes had looked up at me from under Bill Halsey's cowboy hat any number of times.

226

I had brought her an orchid as a small offering of thanks, and I put it on the coffee table as I pulled out one of her notes that I had saved. I thought it might help explain my visit. This one read:

Thank you for your help and love for the HOMELESS and the needy. Pray that God will multiply [sic] this small amount. Pray for me.

As I handed her the note, I could see she understood and remembered writing it. I tried speaking, "Mrs. Halsey, I'm Kathy Izard. You used to send me those notes—"

Mrs. Halsey's friend interrupted. "You need to speak loudly, dear. She can't hear well."

I realized that Lily was still searching my face and had not heard a word. I leaned down close and put my words of gratitude right next to her ear.

"Mrs. Halsey, I'm Kathy Izard. You used to send me those notes, and I wanted to tell you how much they mattered. They meant the world to me."

I tried not to cry, but my throat was closing, and my eyes were welling. It felt good to finally be at the end of this journey. This long road that began with Denver was now ending with a woman I had never met but who had profoundly impacted my life too.

Lily Halsey was crying as well. A tear rolled down her cheek, and she said softly, "Oh, I used to pray for you. I still do. I prayed this morning for you and Moore Place."

We visited for an hour. With the help of her friend, whom I found out had worked with Lily at an advertising agency in Charlotte, she told me things I never knew about her son.

Before he became a fixture at the Urban Ministry Center, Bill was a college graduate and talented artist. He worked for years as a graphic designer. I almost laughed when she told me. Bill? A graphic designer? The same profession I had given up to begin this project.

Bill and I had both learned how to create layouts by hand before computers became so ubiquitous in the industry. Once the profession demanded computer skills, it was difficult to make the transition. I took classes at the community college and finally hired a private tutor to teach me the more advanced software.

Bill hadn't been as lucky. He couldn't afford a tutor. He didn't know he could take classes at the community college. Bill couldn't compete in the digital world. He lost his job, his confidence, and everything after that was a slow slide to desperation. His father died, and the family lost contact with Bill when he started living in that hole in the ground. Lily never stopped worrying about the son she loved.

The newspaper articles about the Urban Ministry Center's plans for housing the homeless caught her eye. She didn't know if they would help her son, but she could pray, couldn't she?

When I asked Lily Halsey why she began sending cards to me, she replied with complete certainty, "When I read about Moore Place, I knew I had to help."

Her blue eyes looked straight into mine, and she said with unwavering faith, "No one would have built Moore Place unless they believed God was in it."

———

I texted Coleman that I was on my way but morning traffic was making me a little late. It was November 8, 2017, and I was picking up Coleman to take him to our eleventh annual True Blessings luncheon. It had been ten years since that group of friends brought Ron and Denver to Charlotte, hoping a few people would attend.

And it had been ten years since we learned that all of the good we were doing during the day wasn't enough. We needed to end homelessness, not just comfort the people who were experiencing it.

Along with Moore Place, we now housed more than 160 other men and women in apartments throughout the city as part of our Housing Works program. We had learned to partner with landlords and use rental subsidy vouchers. In 2015, we had expanded Moore Place to 120 apartments, so now almost 300 people were currently in the program. Between Moore Place and our scattered-site program, the UMC had a better than 90 percent housing retention rate. The City of Charlotte had even formed a coalition of more than thirty agencies into a program called Housing First with a goal to end chronic homelessness. In less than three years the group had jointly housed almost 600 people.

The True Blessings event had grown as well. Eugene Coleman would be giving the blessing for more than twelve hundred people— our biggest year ever with more than forty corporate donors. Since 2007, True Blessings had become Charlotte's largest event for the homeless and in ten years had raised more than $7 million.

Coleman now lived in a one-story apartment on a quiet street, which that day was glowing with yellow and red fall leaves. The last time I saw him, I told him that I was finally finishing that book I was writing. It had taken six years, and I wasn't sure he remembered I had asked for permission to tell his story. I was hoping he was still comfortable with the idea. We were meeting for breakfast, so I brought a sample copy of the book with me.

I put it on the table between us and pushed it toward him. "You remember I told you I was going to write that book?"

He placed his hand on the cover and held it there before looking up at me. "Am I in it?"

"Oh, you are in it!" I told him.

Coleman was quiet for a moment, staring down at the three hundred pages between us. Finally he said, "You remember when I spoke to those high school kids?"

"Yes!" I said. "That story is in there!"

"It is?" he asked, absorbing it all. "You know now that for all the rest of my life, I will know that I am seen."

We both teared up and were silent together, not saying anything. Then he announced, "I think this is about to go viral!"

I laughed, now remembering his words that day, and texted Coleman that I was in front of his apartment. I could see he was dressed to impress in a tan jacket over a sweater and nice slacks. When he got into my car, he was rubbing his hands together nervously, but he held no notes.

"I know what I want to say," he said. "I went to the UMC yesterday and met with Dale to give me advice. He told me there's all kinds of folks coming, so best not mention Jesus."

That made me smile. I knew Coleman leaned toward Christianity.

We caught up during our ride to the event and arrived a little early for a sound check. As we were passing by a coffee shop, I asked Coleman if he wanted anything. He hesitated but then saw a sign advertising the fall special and smiled wide. "Yes! This will be my first pumpkin spice latte of the season!"

During the sound check, Coleman spoke softly and needed several prompts to speak louder. I hoped this was not going to be too big of an assignment for him. He finally got the stage manager's approval, and we found two seats in the ballroom as the convention staff filled water glasses, folded napkins, and set out silverware around us. I pulled out a photo I had uncovered the day before in one of my photo albums and handed it to Coleman. He grinned widely as he looked at it. "Oh man, I remember that day!" he said.

The photo was Coleman on his first day of housing ten years

ago. We had just handed him a key to his new apartment, and he was unlocking the door to his first home in twenty years. He had turned to look at the camera in disbelief as he unlocked the door.

"You don't know how many nights I lay under the moon thinking about just that day and thinking it was so far away, that it would never come," he said.

"Joann clearly remembers talking to you that first day," I told him. "She came right into my office afterward and told me 'this guy is special!'"

"It was the strangest thing," he confided. "I just heard this little voice say to me to go talk to that lady, and I didn't know her, but it was Joann. It was like there was this little angel on my shoulder saying I should go, pushing me. Led me straight to her."

An hour later the lights dimmed, and Coleman and I made our way to the stage. I welcomed the crowd and introduced him. Approaching the lectern, Coleman leaned into the microphone just as we had practiced, but he had not rehearsed a word of what he was about to say.

"I was gettin' nervous about speakin' at this thing," he said. "But then I got to thinkin' these are my friends. They the ones that helped me. I thought love was gone for me, but then here I got a house. You people helped me. You got me off the street. So nah, I ain't nervous! I wanted to do this for all you gave me."

Then he stepped away from the podium and opened the sides of his jacket showing off "his self" with a big smile. "Here you are, this here is Mr. Coleman!"

He then prayed for the food and the people in the room, asking the Lord's blessing on all. Especially those still waiting to be housed. I thought about how far we had come in those ten years. From serving soup to saving lives. Coleman could never have been here in that moment without that shift. Here was Coleman, ten years later blessing those who gave him a second chance and proving that not only does housing work but we need to do more.

Watching Coleman in front of that crowd, it was hard for me to remember how we saw it any other way. It was hard to remember a time when I didn't think homes were the most important thing we could do.

I remembered the dream Coleman had shared with me while we waited for him to give the blessing in the ballroom. "When I went to go to see Dale yesterday, to get some advice on how to say this blessing, I saw all the folks waiting in line," he said.

The UMC still served a meal 365 days a year and was still open for services for those experiencing homelessness.

Coleman looked at me. "And I thought, wouldn't it be a really great day if one day I go down there and nobody's there?"

It took a minute for me to realize what he meant.

"Wouldn't that be great?" he asked again. "If one day, there was nobody there?"

twenty-six

TRUST THE WHISPER

Listen to your life. See it for the fathomless mystery that
it is. In the boredom and pain of it no less than in the
excitement and gladness: touch, taste, smell your way
to the holy hidden heart of it because in the last analysis
all moments are key moments, and life itself is grace.

—Frederick Buechner[1]

I always believed Moore Place was the end game. For years I thought
my purpose started the day I met Denver and would end the day we
opened the doors to that dream of a building. But just as I eventually
learned everything started way before Denver, I now understand it
continues after Moore Place as well. The road keeps going. Moore
Place was one stop on a path that stretches too far ahead for me to
see. If I keep listening, my life is still talking to me.

What was I supposed to do with all that knowledge about building and fundraising? Not be afraid to do it again.

A year and a half after Moore Place opened, a friend, Betsy Blue, asked if I would talk to her about a project she and her husband were feeling called to lead. Their family had experienced mental illness and found it nearly impossible to get care. Although she was an event planner and her husband, Bill, a banker, and neither had any formal psychiatric or medical training, they felt compelled to help all the families in Charlotte struggling with mental illness. The overwhelming need kept whispering to them.

"Did you know there are 7.4 million people within a hundred miles of Charlotte and not a single residential mental health treatment bed?" Betsy asked.

I could almost hear Denver say again, "Does that make any sense to you?"

It didn't.

I knew how difficult it was to have a parent cycle in and out of hospitals. And Charlie and I had just experienced the pain of trying to get help for a child with depression.

Betsy didn't have to ask the next question: "Are you going to do something about it?"

Charlie and I decided to work on this one together, and this time I did not lead.

We walked alongside Bill and Betsy Blue as they spearheaded a community effort to raise $25 million to build HopeWay, the region's first and only nonprofit residential mental health treatment center. What began with five families who had experienced mental illness grew to more than two hundred who made donations to purchase and renovate a twelve-acre campus. In December 2016, four years after Moore Place opened, HopeWay began serving hundreds of clients and families through best-practice residential and day-treatment programs.

As I was working to raise money for HopeWay, I wrote and

rewrote versions of this book. Witnessing Bill and Betsy, listening to their call, I was reminded of all the people who were part of the Moore Place journey. Liz, Dale, Bill Holt, Jerry Licari, and so many more who heard that small whisper to do something—then did it. I didn't want all those stories to be lost. I didn't want to forget how all of this might not have happened if even a few people had not acted on what they heard, no matter how crazy it seemed.

It is difficult to make sense of it all. Life seems completely random and perfectly designed at the same time. Louise sent me a sermon she wrote that said in part:

> If it's all constructed, we might as well write a story large enough to live in. An adventurous story—one where we are joyful, creative, and connected. One where we name ourselves as powerful, willing, and able to offer deep service, available for passionate living. One where we thrive instead of merely survive.

More than anything, that is the gift of the past ten years—the ability to rewrite my story. One where I am connected to a community of friends willing to work for change. One where my history with my mother is not filled with resentment but with compassion. One where my life has a faith found, not forced. And one where, when I pay attention, God definitely shows off.

I no longer believe a calling is reserved exclusively for people like Dale or Louise who go into the ministry. I believe, now, we are each called to life—true, abundant, purposeful life.

Each of us has a call patiently waiting and whispering. You might have heard yours already but are afraid to admit it. It could be as big as a building, as technical as creating proformas for a non-profit, or as simple and powerful as a ministry of sending cards.

My message to you is this: trust the whisper.

Whatever it is. Whatever you feel is quietly, persistently, relent-lessly calling to you. No matter how crazy or inconvenient it might be to listen.

Once you hear it, that one true thing, it's impossible to turn away because it will keep whispering. And when it does, you must spend the rest of your life either answering it or pretending you never heard it.

Be willing to listen.

Be willing to let go.

Be willing to take that leap of faith.

When you do, the life you can't see is infinitely richer and more significant than the life you can see and thought you had planned.

The day I took a ride with Denver, he took me to a road that wasn't even on my map. I hope your journey begins today and leads you to a path you never thought capable of navigating.

I can't explain grace or God's plan, but this much I have learned: grace is that moment when your purpose speaks to you so loudly you can't help but hear it. Believing in it is crazy, but denying you heard it is even crazier. You may not see it coming, but when grace finds you, stop, listen, and take good notes. Everything in your life has prepared you for this.

You are ready, and grace is real.

THE LAST WORD

Although some names in *The Hundred Story Home* were changed to protect the privacy of individuals, the one name I regret I could not change was my mother's. That would have been her preference. After the long sixteen-year search for the right medication and treatment, Mom has lived the past thirty as many patients do—in silence and secrecy about her circumstances because of the pervasive stigma surrounding mental illness.

My mother's bipolar diagnosis did not and does not define her life. It merely became one facet she learned to manage. Mom never wanted a career because her singular goal in life was to be a mother. She wanted to expose her three daughters to each of the arts she loves so much: painting, music, dance, opera.

During her struggles and after, Mom was always determined that her life would mean something. She was instrumental in establishing the Girls Club of El Paso, which she served in several roles, including president, volunteer coordinator, and program coordinator. First Presbyterian Church has also been a main focus of her service where she has been a deacon, an elder, and a faithful choir member. Her passion for reading makes her a dedicated member of two book clubs, the Fantastiks and Tuesday Book Club. Her favorite activity each week, however, remains her Wednesday bridge group, with whom she has laughed and shared stories for more than twenty years. Mom has always believed that the three sustaining pillars of her life are faith, family, and friends.

Mental illness affects one in five adults in a given year, and everyone knows someone who has struggled with a mental health issue: anxiety, depression, and addiction to name a few. I pray that the final message of this book is to know treatment and hope are available. Let's end the stigma and start talking about mental health with the same normalcy we extend to physical health. That is something we all can do.

Here are some mental health resources:

IN CHARLOTTE:
HopeWay
www.hopewayfoundation.org

NATIONAL:
National Alliance on Mental Illness (NAMI)
www.nami.org

Bring Change 2 Mind
A nonprofit organization working to end the stigma and discrimination surrounding mental illness.
www.bringchange2mind.org

READER'S GUIDE

Thank you for reading *The Hundred Story Home: A Memoir of Finding Faith in Ourselves and Something Bigger.* I would love to be in your living room discussing this with you, your book club, or study group. Below are some questions to get the conversation going. If you have discussed *The Hundred Story Home*, let me know! I'm eager to hear your responses, including related issues your group discussed that weren't in this guide. Send your comments and suggestions to kathy@kathyizard.com.

1. One of the central themes in *The Hundred Story Home* is homelessness, yet there are many levels to this issue, from those living on the streets to the challenge of eldercare. Have you ever experienced homelessness or even a temporary loss of place or self? In what ways could you relate to people like Samuel, Jay, Ruth, and Coleman? Have you had to move parents from their home?

2. Did getting to know the stories of how people like Coleman and Chilly Willy became homeless make you feel or think differently about homelessness or homeless people? Do you ever feel compelled to stop and talk to a homeless person and learn his or her story? Have you? If not, what holds you back?

3. How did the stories of women like Christine (who left the pilot program) affect your perspective about how homelessness might be different for women than men?

4. Mental illness is a prevalent theme in *The Hundred Story Home*. It carries a similar stigma to homelessness. Although one in five adults will be diagnosed in a given year with a mental illness, a silence and perceived shame around the topic remain. The National Association on Mental Illness encourages people to "see the person, not the illness." Do you or someone you love have experience with this type of stigma? How does it make you feel? What are some ways we can reach out to people who might be suffering in this way?

5. I wrote that I was raised not to be good, but to Do Good. Along with the lesson from my grandmother to Love Well, these messages became driving forces in my life and influenced how Charlie and I raised our daughters. What were you raised to believe, and how have those beliefs influenced your life (and if you have children, your parenting)? What beliefs would you like to keep? Which would you like to change?

6. In *The Hundred Story Home*, I had rejected religion but discovered I actually had a defining belief in faith. Was there a time in your life when you felt religion, faith, or spirituality was not for you? Has that changed? If so, what experiences led you to change?

7. The idea of renewal and rebirth also recurs in the story, from the junkyard that became a home, to each homeless person housed, to my mother's affinity with the symbol of the Phoenix. Have you ever been given a second chance? Was there a time in your life when you felt you reinvented yourself to leave something old behind?

8. The homeless tend to be an invisible part of society. Coleman asked the high school audience if they could see him because for years on the streets, he believed nobody could. Also, I couldn't *see* the problem with giving people just soup and programs until Denver made me see it differently. Have you had experience with something invisible suddenly made visible to you? What changed your vision?

9. I often felt guilty for having lived a relatively privileged life. How do you think our social class affects how we see the world? Have you felt uncomfortable with your class or perceived status of having too much or too little?

10. Throughout my journey I experienced "God-instances": circumstances so unexpected that it seemed unlikely they were coincidental and not connected to something divine. Do you agree? Have you ever had a God-instance in your life? How did you explain it?

11. I didn't want or expect homelessness to be my purpose because it seemed to be such a huge, overwhelming problem. I needed to connect with a community that was already doing something about it. Are you passionate about a cause or an issue affecting your community? How have you acted on that interest? If you haven't, what's holding you back? Is there a nonprofit you could help or a community you could join that is working for a goal that interests you?

FREQUENTLY ASKED
BOOK CLUB QUESTIONS

The Hundred Story Home first came out in a self-published paper-back. As friends read it, they suggested it to their book clubs, and I started going on guest appearances. As friends passed it to friends, I went to book clubs all over Charlotte, the surrounding area, and even to friends out of town. The discussions would vary depending on the group, but many questions would be similar. Some of the top recurring questions are answered here.

How long did it take to write the book, and did you take writing classes?

Writing this book began with a New Year's Eve resolution to myself in 2010. I vowed that in 2011, I would write something longer than an e-mail. Throughout that year I worked on a first draft, trying to capture all the miracles of Moore Place—the many God-instances that I just couldn't believe. It really started out as more of a timeline of stories than a book. After working on it a year, I finally let Charlie read the first draft. He told me truthfully, "Honey, it's not a page-turner." Ouch. He was right.

I didn't want a good story to be lost in a bad book, so I decided to take some courses at Queen's University—where my mother went to college. Between 2012 and 2015, I took three courses. The first one was on finding your voice and storytelling; the second was a crash course in writing a manuscript in a month, just to practice getting words on paper; the third was editing an entire book over a semester. That third class was what changed this book completely. In that course twelve aspiring authors were paired with four editors in New York. Over the semester we would get the chance to really dig into our manuscripts and make them shine. My editor in that course, Emily Bell, told me, "No one is going to care about this story unless they care about you. You have to write about you." When I told her there was no way I was writing about me or my childhood since my whole family never talked about it and pretended it never happened, she wouldn't give in. Instead, she proposed this: "For the sake of argument, let's pretend no one is ever going to read this book. What would you write if no one was ever going to read it?"

That was how this book was born.

Where did you get the quotes at the beginning of the chapters?

I have always loved reading and will underline quotes and save passages from books. I still love holding a book and writing in the margins, so I don't read eBooks. When I started writing in 2011, I created a document on my computer and would type in some of my favorites quotes from books for inspiration. I began a habit of cutting and pasting a quote at the beginning of a chapter to be my guiding theme as I wrote that section. Sometimes, as the chapter would evolve, the quote no longer fit, so I would find a new one that fit the revisions.

As I got closer to finishing and publishing, I became more insecure about putting my writing into the world, worried that I didn't have anything to say. I decided I would leave the quotes in as a gift to the reader. If readers didn't like my writing, at least they would get over twenty good quotes for the price of the book!

You write very openly about yourself in this book. How hard was it to put so much of your childhood in this story?

This was one of the most difficult parts of writing this book. I have said it took two editors and two therapists to finish *The Hundred Story Home*—that is the truth! When I started writing this, I was forty-eight and had never really processed my childhood experiences. It had been much easier to just put all those feelings in a box and pretend they didn't happen. But in writing and trying to understand what had happened with Denver, I had to open all those boxes. I had to figure out who was I, that when a formerly home-less man whom I had never met tells me that I should build beds, I listen? I needed to go back and figure out why I felt what he said so deeply. I knew all that had to do with how I was raised and who my parents were. To tell this story, I was going to have to explore my story, and to do that, I was going to have to write about my mom.

For four years I wrote and never let anyone read it and never intended to publish it. But I started liking what I was writing, and by that time I was working every day on HopeWay. As I wrote briefly toward the end of the book, building Moore Place led to working on the capital campaign for HopeWay, a nonprofit residential mental health treatment center in Charlotte. I had said I would never raise money for anything again after Moore Place, but suddenly I had agreed to chair raising the money for something else that was even closer to my heart.

At night and on weekends I worked on this book, but in the day I was having conversations about mental illness all the time. Several times a week I would meet with families and foundations who had a connection to mental health, explaining what we were trying to build.

The conversations quickly turned to their own personal stories, usually with much different endings than my mother's story—addiction, suicide, tremendous pain and suffering. I started to see not only was this a problem in one in five families but also how very fortunate we were that my mother had turned to the Bible, not the bottle, to handle her struggles. Her faith and strength were amazing. We were also so lucky to have strong family support throughout it all.

By the time the book was finished, the mental health portion of my story was no longer the dark secret it had been. It felt much healthier to talk about it and say what happened than hide it anymore.

What should I do when I see someone asking for money on the street? How do I know whether someone is really homeless or a con artist?

As someone who has worked in homeless services, I should tell you to ask them if they know of resources in your community and direct them to appropriate agencies. As an individual who knows how difficult that can be, I will tell you what Dale Mullennix taught me, "Err on the side of compassion." I don't give to every person I see asking for money or food. But there are certain times when someone just tugs at my heart in a way I can't explain, and in those cases, I give what I feel is right. I have learned that everyone has a story, so I try not to judge why someone might be holding up a sign. If I don't have any dollars, I try to at least look someone in the eye and let them know they are seen. I know from Eugene Coleman what a difference that can make, just to make someone feel human. A kind word or a smile might give someone the hope he or she needs to make it one more day.

What do you hope readers take from your book?

I have two hopes for this book. First, I hope *The Hundred Story*

Home is a bridge book into faith for some people. I know the world can be very divided in terms of people's views of religion and God. From people who believe in nothing to those who are certain of their beliefs. If you are questioning your faith, it can be difficult to find where you belong. I hope this book encourages people who have given up on God, for whatever reason, to reexamine their beliefs. The second hope is that in reading my story, readers will have faith and courage to answer their own call—whatever that might be. I was so unprepared and unqualified to take on building a building. But once I started trusting that there was something bigger than me going on, it was much easier to find the people who were also drawn to this cause. I definitely now believe that those whispers we want to ignore are our best guides for living life. I hope my book amplifies those whispers that people are already hearing.

ACKNOWLEDGMENTS

At least a hundred stories make up Moore Place. Some are told in these pages, but countless others, and the people who are a part of them, are not. If yours is a story I didn't tell, please know you are part of the fabric of Moore Place, and I am so grateful for your help and presence along this journey. I am particularly indebted to the following people:

Charlie, the First Believer. My Goose.

Lauren, Kailey, Emma, and Maddie, thank you for all your love, patience, and support from the first True Blessings to the doorknob. No words.

Louise, my oracle, for being there from the beginning through every otherworldly happening.

Dad, for making me believe I could do anything.

Mom, for your daily courage and for starting the journey I never saw coming.

Bob and Jean, for being the first donors to the dream and loving me as your own.

Allyson, for being my first best friend and helping me find the words written inside.

Karen Green Pirinelli, for being the first Green Girl to discover *Same Kind of Different As Me*.

Ann and Rolfe Neill, for bringing me to Charlotte, where this story began.

Liz Clasen-Kelly, for being the passionate voice that always knew what this city needed to do.

Dale Mullennix, for giving this Graphics Girl a chance and for doing the really hard work every day for over two decades.

John and Pat Moore, for your daring belief that every human being deserves a home.

Sarah Belk, Angela Breeden, Kim Belk, Edwina Willis Fleming, Paige Waugh, Karen Pritchett, and Paige James, for the First True Blessings that started it all.

Libba Rule, Christe Eades, Barb Singer, Mary Katherine Black, Addison Ayer, and all those who have kept True Blessings running strong since 2007.

Caroline Chambre Hammock, for leaving New York and making Moore Place your home.

Joann Markley, for believing in this with me and keeping the first thirteen safe.

The original Homeless to Homes tenants, for having the courage to be first and showing what was possible.

Eugene Coleman, for sharing your story and making me believe in angels.

Jennie Buckner, for having the courage to lead the change on our mission.

Rich Hoard, Megan Coffey, Liz Peralta, Lauren Cranford, Trish Fries, and Beth Galen, for your dedication to this work, which made Moore Place possible.

Bill Holt, Hugh McColl III, Downie Saussy, Matt Wall, and Jerry Licari (the Five Guys), for doing everything I couldn't and more.

Gary Chesson, Mike Clement, and Greg Gach, for your leadership in changing hearts and minds.

David Furman and Steve Barton, for taking a sketch on a napkin and translating it into an amazing home.

Laura Schulte, for saying the improbable, impossible, biggest yes, and Jay Everette, for everything else.

Mike Rizer, for being the miracle maker behind the scenes.

Anthony Foxx, for championing what was right even when people thought it was wrong.

Paul Walker, Lori Thomas, and Susan Furtney, for creating the plan that would make the vision of Moore Place possible.

Louise Parsons, Sally Saussy, Anne Fehring, Angela Breeden, Tricia Harrison, and Barb Singer, for making each room a home.

Jan Shealy, for keeping track of every dollar and every name, and Tommy Shealy, for his leadership in the campaign.

Zelleka Beirman, for putting heart and soul into city policy.

Mary Reca Todd, for her career of compassion with the state of North Carolina.

Tammie Lesesne, for listening and showing me how to live in the gray.

Heidi Rotberg, for teaching me there are no magic wands or crystal balls, and forgiveness is a good thing.

Chip Edens, for encouraging me to take a leap of faith.

Lisa Saunders, for helping me believe.

Lynn Pearce Tate, for keeping me in her prayers and helping me believe in my own.

The Schpilkies, for fifteen years of friendship and helping me imagine the unimaginable.

Mary Beth Hollet, for encouraging me to write this book, and especially for pushing me to She Speaks.

Liza Branch, Julie Marr, Renee McColl, and Kathleen Richardson, for two decades of keeping it real and always reminding Sister Mary Margaret to do the same, and for supporting every dream.

Sandra Conway, for the walks and talks that inspired No Casseroles for Crazy.

Edwina Willis Fleming, for the words I carry in my wallet, and for not letting me forget.

Jane Harrell, for making me comfortable with this whole God thing and so much more.

Julie Marr, for being my spiritual director, encouraging me to Tell About It, and writing a genius title.

Betsy and Bill Blue, for inviting me on their journey and showing me how grace continues to lead.

Lisa Cashion, for showing me the new dream and where this road goes next.

Emily Bell, for making me dig even deeper than I ever wanted to go.

Peg Robarchek, for encouraging me that this may be good enough, and for reading my first bad drafts.

My beta readers: Kristin Hills Bradberry, Carrie Banwell, Beth Gast, Susan Izard, Gigi Priebe, and Nancy Engen (with her canasta club: Susie Davis, Erin Lamb, and Susan Wasilauskas), for giving me the confidence to take this manuscript out of a drawer.

My digital marketing team: Lauren and Kailey Izard, Corrie Smith, Morgan Bailey, Susan Walker, and Emily Brinkley, for helping launch this story into the world.

Jon Valk, Karen Minster, Fiona Hallowell, and Diane Aronson, for making the first version of this book beautiful.

Rachel Estes and Melissa Leahey, for being the first out-of-town believers.

Meg Robertson, who flew into my life through a Tai Chi studio window and has given me otherworldly courage ever since.

Sally McMillan, for being the final God-instance in this story, and for believing it could be bigger.

ACKNOWLEDGMENTS

Daisy Hutton, for being the last, best editor and knowing exactly what this book needed.

Erin Healy, Paula Major, and the Thomas Nelson team for polishing this story and helping me take it so much further than I could on my own.

The staff and volunteers at Urban Ministry Center and Moore Place, for showing up 365 days a year to love thy Neighbor.

The 259 donors to Moore Place, for bringing us home.

NOTES

CHAPTER 1: SIX CANDLES, ONE WISH
1. Richard Rohr, *Falling Upward: A Spirituality for the Two Halves of Life* (Hoboken, NJ: Jossey-Bass, 2011), 84.

CHAPTER 2: DO GOOD. LOVE WELL.
1. Pico Iyer, *Falling Off the Map: Some Lonely Places of the World* (New York: Knopf Doubleday, 2011), 9.

CHAPTER 3: NO CASSEROLES FOR CRAZY
1. Frederick Buechner, *Beyond Words: Daily Readings in the ABC's of Faith* (New York: HarperOne, 2004), 139.

CHAPTER 4: HEADED FOR HOME
1. Charles de Lint, *The Blue Girl* (Toronto: Penguin, 2006), 127.

CHAPTER 5: A HEART WITH A HOLE
1. Elizabeth Stone in *I'll Fly Away: Further Testimonies from the Women of York Prison*, ed. Wally Lamb (New York: Harper, 2007), 55.

CHAPTER 6: SOUP AND SALVATION
1. Antoine de Saint-Exupéry, *The Little Prince* (New York: Houghton Mifflin Harcourt, 2000), 63.

CHAPTER 7: FAILURE IS NOT AN OPTION
1. Shauna Niequist, *Bittersweet: Thoughts on Change, Grace, and Learning the Hard Way* (Grand Rapids: Zondervan, 2013), 54.

CHAPTER 8: WORKING MY WAY HOME

1. Wayne Muller, *A Life of Being, Having and Doing Enough* (New York: Harmony, 2011), 228.

CHAPTER 9: GOING FOR A RIDE

1. W. Somerset Maugham, in Suzanne Horton, Louise Beattie, and Branwen Bingle, *Lessons in Teaching Reading Comprehension in Primary Schools* (Los Angeles: Learning Matters, 2015), 10.

CHAPTER 10: HOME TOUR

1. Anne Lamott, *Traveling Mercies: Some Thoughts on Faith* (New York: Anchor Books, 2006), 143.

CHAPTER 11: MILLION-DOLLAR LARRY

1. C. S. Lewis, "Miracles," sermon, St. Jude on the Hill Church, London, November 26, 1942, in *God in the Dock* (Grand Rapids: William B. Eerdmans, 2014), 13.

CHAPTER 12: WING AND A PRAYER

1. Thomas Merton, *Conjectures of a Guilty Bystander* (New York: Image Books, 2009), 206.

CHAPTER 13: TRASH AND TREASURE

1. Anna Quindlen, *Lots of Candles, Plenty of Cake: A Memoir of a Woman's Life* (New York: Random House, 2012), 87.

CHAPTER 14: PRAYING TO A GOD YOU DON'T BELIEVE IN

1. *The Great God Brown*, 4.1, in Eugene O'Neill, *Selected Letters of Eugene O'Neill* (New York: Limelight, 1994), 264n2.

CHAPTER 15: HOME ALONE

1. James Baldwin, *Giovanni's Room* (New York: Vintage International, 2013), 92.

CHAPTER 16: CHRISTMAS MIRACLES

1. Becca Stevens, *Love Heals*, Thistle Farms, December 11, 2013.

CHAPTER 17: PAPERS AND PRAYERS

1. Mary Oliver, "The Summer Day," in *New and Selected Poems*, vol. 1 (Boston: Beacon Press, 2004), 94.

CHAPTER 18: THE FIRST YES

1. Paulo Coelho, *The Alchemist*, trans. Alan R. Clarke (New York: HarperOne, 2015), 64.

CHAPTER 19: CRAZY OR CALLED

1. John Newton, "Amazing Grace," 1779.

CHAPTER 20: GIFTS FROM ABOVE

1. Joseph Campbell, *Reflections on the Art of Living: A Joseph Campbell Companion*, ed. Diane K. Osbon (New York: Harper Perennial, 1995), 18.

CHAPTER 21: BLESS AND MULTIPLY THIS SMALL AMOUNT

1. Lauren Kate, *Torment* (New York: Delacorte Press, 2010), 358.

CHAPTER 22: JUST LISTEN

1. Ann Patchett, *State of Wonder* (New York: HarperCollins, 2011), 246.

CHAPTER 23: THE LAST, BEST YES

1. Elisabeth Kubler-Ross, *Death: The Final Stage of Growth* (New York: Simon and Schuster, 2008), 96.

CHAPTER 24: I FEEL LIKE PEOPLE NOW

1. Haruki Murakami, *Kafka on the Shore* (New York: Vintage, 2006), 5.

CHAPTER 25: GOD WAS IN IT

1. John Irving, *A Prayer for Owen Meany* (New York: William Morrow, 2013), 458.
2. 1 Corinthians 13:13.

CHAPTER 26: TRUST THE WHISPER

1. Frederick Buechner, *Listening to Your Life: Daily Meditations with Frederick Buechner*, January 1 (New York: HarperOne, 1992), 2.

ABOUT THE AUTHOR

KATHY IZARD was an award-winning graphic designer for twenty years in Charlotte before launching the pilot program Homeless to Homes for the Urban Ministry Center in 2007. She successfully demonstrated this Housing First program could succeed and led the city-wide effort to build Moore Place, Charlotte's first permanent supportive housing for chronically homeless men and women. Kathy has worked on numerous civic projects, most recently leading the development campaign for HopeWay, Charlotte's first nonprofit residential mental health treatment center. She is the recipient of the Bank of America Local Hero Award and the NC Housing Volunteer of the Year Award. She, her husband, and four daughters have made Charlotte their home for more than thirty years.

For more information, please visit
www.kathyizard.com

WANT TO KNOW MORE?

Photos, videos, and reader resources are available at
www.kathyizard.com

LIKE THE BOOK?
WANT TO RECOMMEND IT?

Please take a moment to post a quick review on
Amazon or Goodreads and let people know what
you thought of *The Hundred Story Home*.

Thank you for purchasing this book.
The author will donate a portion of her
earnings in the sale of this book to
Moore Place and the Urban Ministry Center
in Charlotte, North Carolina.
If you want to learn more or donate directly online,
please visit
www.urbanministrycenter.org.